I0817936

INDO-JUDAIC PARALLELS

INDO-JUDAIC PARALLELS

Notes on Similar Motifs in Judaism and Hinduism

DANIEL SPERBER

URIM PUBLICATIONS
Jerusalem · New York

Indo-Judaic Parallels:
Notes on Similar Motifs in Judaism and Hinduism

by Daniel Sperber

Typeset by Juliet Tresgallo

Printed in Israel

First Edition

ISBN 978-965-524-366-6

Cover design by the Virtual Paintbrush

Urim Publications
P.O. Box 52287
Jerusalem 9152102 Israel

www.UrimPublications.com

Cataloging-in-Publication data is available from the Library of Congress.

Contents

Introductory Note

When idly perusing various writings on Hindu myths, practices, and folkloristic rituals, I was frequently reminded of apparent parallels in our own Jewish sources.[1] So I started collecting somewhat random notes on little

1. Clearly, I am by no means the first or only person to note such apparent parallels. Some I have already noted in this introduction, and doubtless there are many more. Thus, recently I came upon Verrier Elwin's *Folk-Tales of Mahakoshal*, Oxford University Press, 1944, where he discusses the motif of "the act of truth," referring to *2 Kings* 1:10–12, where Elijah calls down fire from heaven, if he be "a man of God," and Verrier brings numerous parallels with bibliography from Indian sources (pp. 186–188). Similarly, ibid., pp. 160–161, 181–184, we read of divination by shooting arrows (referring to S. Hislop, *Papers Relating to the Aboriginal Tribes of the Central Provinces*, Nagpur 1866, part III, p. 17), which parallels a famous passage in *B. Gittin* 56a, where we read that the Emperor Nero shoots arrows in various directions to clarify whether he will be successful in battle. (I imagine there are classical parallels to this, but I have not searched them out. But see Smith's *A Dictionary of Greek and Roman Antiquities*, London, 1880, vol. 1, p. 606, s.v. Divinatio; Daremberg and Saglio, *Dictionnaire des Antiquités Grecques et Romaines*, vol. 2, Paris, 1892, s.v. Divinatio, pp. 292, 319.) See also *B. Sanhedrin* 19b on placing a sword between man and woman as a sign of chastity (see L. Ginzberg, *The Legends of the Jews*, vol. 6, Philadelphia, 1926, pp. 273–274, note 133; citing Haller REJ 49, p. 190, "that the legend is dependent on Indian sources," and cf. Elwin, ibid., p. 35, in a Baiga story from Rewa State).

   Similarly the Jonah story, where he is swallowed by a fish and lives there for a while in the fish's belly (also paralleled in part in Lucian, *Vera Historia* I), has parallels in India; see Elwin, ibid., pp. 64–65; see also N. H. Penzer, *The Ocean of Story*, vol. 6, London, 1926, p. 15.

   Prof. David Flusser, in an article entitled "Abraham and the Upanishads," in

pieces of paper, which I have now collected together and put in some kind of order. I have made no attempt to analyze these similarities or to seek any kind of intercultural influences in either direction, with the exception of a few cases. Many of these comparisons have numerous parallels in other geographic and cultural areas and they may well have merely a structural similarity. I have purposely avoided dealing with any of the subjects so ably discussed by Barbara A. Holdrege in her masterful study *Veda and Torah: Transcending the Textuality of Scripture*, State University of New York, 1996. Likewise, I have not discussed many and diverse themes so widely found in a variety of cultures, such as menstrual impurity, the holding of hands at a marriage ceremony, and/or tying the couple's clothes together, because of their almost universal dissemination and obvious symbolic roots.[2] Similarly, I have not discussed the theme of the scapegoat found in the Bible (*Leviticus* 16:6–20), to which J. G. Frazer dictated a whole volume of his *The Golden Bough* (vol. 9, entitled "The Scapegoat," 1913).[3]

Clearly the reader will raise the question as to whether this material is the result of intercultural influence[4] or "spontaneous generation of

---

his volume *Judaism and the Origins of Christianity*, Jerusalem, 1988, pp. 645–653, noted the similarity between the Abrahamic parable in *Genesis Rabba* 39:1, p. 365, and what we read in the *Panchantantra* 3:9, transl. Edgerton, Delhi, 1975, pp. 127–128, transl. Benfeys, Berlin, 1859, pp. 376–377.

2. See what I wrote in my *The Jewish Life Cycle*, vol. 2, chapter 20, entitled "On Dextrum Iunctio," and add: R. E. Enthoven, *Tribes and Castes of Bombay*, vol. 2, 1922, pp. 50, 52–53, 57, etc.; E. Thurston, *Castes and Tribes of Southern India*, vol. 1, Madras, 1909, pp. 234, 265, 281, etc., vol. 3, pp. 236, 481, etc., vol. 5, p. 37, etc.

3. And see, for example, Thurston, ibid., vol. 1, p. 116, where the Bagadas' sin is transferred to a calf, after which it is let loose and may never be used for secular work.

4. There are, of course, examples where both the source and the direction of influence are preeminently clear, even though radical changes may have taken place in the process of the "migration." Thus, when J. P. Ferrier and Jesse Williams tell us, in their *Caravan Journeys of 1850*, that there was a practice to nail the ear of a slave who attempted to escape to the door, and even to leave him there for three days

culture in different parts of the world." These two scientific approaches have been most ably categorized in Rudolf Wittkower's introduction to his *Allegory and the Migration of Symbols*, New York, 1977, pp. 10–14, entitled "East and West: The Problem of Cultural Exchange." He summarizes the problem as follows (p. 10):

> For almost a century ethnologists have worked with two antagonistic theories: diffusion of techniques, ideas, concepts, and art forms *versus* independent, 'spontaneous generation' of culture in different parts of the world. These mutually exclusive working methods have been hotly debated ever since A. Bastian, in the second half of the 19th century, propounded his evolutionary thesis that similar cultural characteristics arise at parallel phases in the development of different societies. The advocates of diffusionism and the defenders of independent convergence are still at each other's throats. Their discussions pertain mainly to pre-literary civilizations. For the high civilizations with literary traditions diffusionism has been developed into a universally accepted technique of research; in art-historical controversies the degree and character of diffusion may be debated, but the principle of diffusion is not called into question.
>
> The historian of culture or art who, through the study of high civilizations, has learned to operate with diffusionist interchanges is more readily prepared than the ethnologist to extend the method to nonliterary, so-called primitive cultures. Nobody can deny that the artifacts of the northern nomad tribes are found distributed over an enormous area, though the precise roads of transmission may never be traceable.
>
> Acceptance of diffusion does not, however, preclude the possibility of convergence and parallelism of cultural phenomena. Certain art forms, which we conventionally designate as archaic,

---

till he died, we obviously will connect this with the biblical ruling to pierce the ear of a slave who does not wish to leave his master with an awl to the doorpost (see *Exodus* 21:5–6; *Deuteromy* 15:16–17).

> classic, baroque, etc., recur in widely separate civilizations at unrelated periods, a sign perhaps of the comparative dearth of basic artistic expressions, the world over, at the disposal of our species.
>
> The ultimate test of diffusion lies, of course, in the proof of the existence of definitely traceable roads of migration. Even in prehistoric times there existed caravan roads bridging the vast expanses of the Asian land-mass between China and Europe, a northern route via the Caspian and Black Seas and a southern route via the highland of Iran and Syria. In historic times, the Romans, who kept the southern road open for hundreds of years, imported much coveted silk from China. Although the road was virtually cut with Arab ascendancy and was reopened only in the middle of the 13th century when the *pax mongolica* had pacified the largest part of Asia, the areas along this road always remained the great melting pot of cultural and artistic currents. But just when the material regarding the roads of transmission is ample, we must sharpen our critical judgment, for the pitfalls of superficial affinities may lead and have led to strange misconceptions.

See his continued discussion, and especially his observation on p. 14:

> There is a large body of cultural material, perhaps best subsumed under the vague terms "symbols" and "archetypal images", that we encounter through long periods of time and wide spaces, the origins of which are lost in the early dawn of history. The gammadion or swastika, the winged globe, the Tree of Life, the eagle and snake, the Great Mother, the mythical hero as animal-tamer, the dragon, and the totemistic fauna of animals and monsters all form part of this material. Scholars who tread this complex territory diverge widely, for the permutations of both type and meaning seem almost infinite. Nevertheless, such symbols no longer elude the persistent and judicious investigator who, by inquiring into their pedigree and history, can often

> throw unexpected light on the give-and-take between East and West.

And he concludes (ibid.), as an art historian, with the following cautionary statement:

> The problem of cultural homogeneity linking Europe and the high civilizations of Asia has many facets. The West and China and Japan share an interest in art produced for edification, meditation, and aesthetic enjoyment, in the representation of the human body and face, in the narrative theme, in nature and the mute objects of our daily life, in the individual artist's self-surrender and emotive experience. At the same time the difference of interpretation of similar themes East and West, as well as similarities of formal approaches potentially embedded in different traditions, cannot be overlooked.[5]

---

5. But, of course, similarity in the structure of a theme does not necessarily posit influence. Thus, for example, the tale of Gunaśarman and Queen Aśokavati who attempts to seduce him, and, when unable to do so, claims he attempted to rape her, etc., related in Somadeva's *Kathā Sarit Sāgara* (in *The Ocean of Story*, transl. C. H. Tawney, ed. N. M. Penzer, vol. 4, London, 1924, pp. 91–96), so similar in many ways to the biblical story of Joseph and Pharaoh's wife in *Genesis* 39 (as noted by William Alexander Clouston in his *Popular Tales and Fictions: Their Migrations and Transformations*, vol. 2, Edinburg and London, 1887, pp. 499–502), certainly does not necessitate positing any sort of mutual influence. See also "Joseph and Potiphar in Hindu Fiction," by M. Bloomfield, in *Transaction of the American Philological Association* 54, 1923, pp. 141–176; A. Stein and G. A. Grierson, *Hatim's Tales, Kashmiri Stories and Songs*, London, 1923, pp. 33–37. And see below section 12.

   On this whole subject see also Joseph Campbell, *the Mythic Image*, Princeton, NJ, 1974, p. 72, referring to James Frazer, *The Golden Bough*, vol. 1, New York, 1922, p. 386, and Campbell's own comments, ibid.

   And to the above we may add Berthold Laufer's fascinating article "The Jonah Legend in India," *The Monist* 18, 1908, pp. 576–578, where despite noting several joint elements, there is no suggestion of sister-cultural transfer.

   And while mentioning that remarkable scholar, we might also take note of his article in the *American Journal of Semitic Languages and Literature*, XLVI/3, April 1930, pp. 189–197, "A Chinese-Hebrew Manuscript: A New Source for the History of Chinese Jews." For on pp. 321–322 he cites two inscriptions, one of 1512, which states that the first ancestor in Adam is traced to India, and the second from 1663

However, in some instances the direct influence of the Bible is clearly evident. Thus Edward Tuite Dalton, in his *Descriptive Ethnology of Bengal*, Calcutta, 1872, when describing the religion of the Kandhs

---

which states that the Jewish religion took "origin in India." He adds that the official destination of Chinese Jews was "religion of India." Presumably this is because Indian Jews came from Persia and Chinese Jews from India.

And as we have mentioned the Jonah story, we might take account of W. A. Clouston's note in Richard F. Burton's *Supplemental Nights*, vol. 2, Benares, 1886, p. 345, note 2:

> This [the above tale] is one of the innumerable parallels to the story of Jonah in the "whale's" belly which occur in Asiatic fictions. See, for some instances, Tawney's translation of the "Kathá Sarit Ságara," chapters xxxv. and lxxiv.; "Indian Antiquary," Sept. 1885, Legend of Ahlá; Miss Stokes' "Indian Fairy Tales," pp. 75, 76; and Steel and Temple's "Wide-Awake Stories from the Panjáb and Kashmir," p. 411. In Lucian's "Vera Historia," a monster fish swallows a ship and her crew, who live a long time in the extensive regions comprised in its internal economy. See also Heritage's "Gseta Romanorum" (Early English Text Society), p. 297.

And cf. ibid., p. 350 and note 3.

And for additional such comments by Clouston, see Burton, vol. 3, Benares, 1887, p. 640, note 2. For a Sinhalese "exact counterpart" to the biblical legend of the widow's cause, and ibid., p. 634, note 3, for a parallel to the biblical crossing of the Dead Sea in a Bengali tale.

We may also call attention to the strange tradition that the tombs of Solomon and David are in the Andaman Islands, according to Captain Buzurg Ibn Shahriyar of Ramhormuz in *The Book of the Wonders of India: Mainland, Sea and Islands*, ed. and transl. G. S. P. Freeman-Grenville, London, 1981, sect. LXXXVII, p. 78. Buzurg died c. 1009, and Ramhormuz is a small town in Khuzistan, some thirty-six miles from Ahwaz. See also Freeman in Paideuma 28, 1982, "Some Thoughts on Buzurg Ibn Shahriyar al-Ramhormuz's The Book of the Wonders of India," and Suhanna Shafiq, *Seafarers of the Seven Seas*, chapter 4, De Gruyter, 2020.

And while we are discussing interesting parallels in Buzurg, we might mention chapter LXXXII, pp. 75–76, where we read of how diamonds are raised from a deep chasm by killing sheep and throwing their bodies into this chasm where diamonds stick to the meat. Vultures then swoop down to the meal, and as they fly up the diamonds fall off the meat to be gathered up by awaiting diamond merchants. This theme is paralleled by both Chinese and Hellenistic folkloric sources, as collected so brilliantly by Berthold Laufer in his *The Diamond: A Study in Chinese and Hellenistic Folklore*, Field Museum of Natural History: Anthropological Series, vol. XV, nos. 1 and 2, Chicago, 1915–17, pp. 6–21, "Legend of the Diamond Valley." As to whether this legend originates in India or elsewhere, see ibid., pp. 15–20.

of southern Bengal, writes on pp. 286–287 that their "system of theocracy … appears to me to be a mélange of Genesis, the several Hindu systems and primitive paganism." He then continues (ibid.) as follows:

> The fundamental doctrines appear to be a belief in a Supreme Being, the source of good, and Creator of the universe, called Bura Penu, the god of light, or Bela Penu, the sun god, the same as the Dharmi of the Oraons and the Bedo Gosain of the Rajmahali highlanders who injured no one, and whom it was not therefore necessary to propitiate, and his wife Tari, who in antagonism to her husband, became the originator of all the ills that befall mankind. We are told that Bura Penu found his wife "wanting in affectionate compliance," which in a note is explained to mean that she declined to scratch his back; but this simple domestic difference put it into Bura Penu's mind to clothe the world with vegetation, fill it with animal life and finally to create human beings to pay him the adoration and veneration which he expected and could not obtain from his wife. Mankind was created exempt from moral and physical evil, and thus enjoyed free intercourse with God. They lived without labour on the spontaneous abundance of the earth in perfect harmony, peace and innocence, and knew not that they were naked till Tari, like the old serpent, filled with envy at their happiness, sowed the seed of sin in their hearts, and like Pandora introduced all the ills that flesh is heir to. A few who withstood temptation and bore up against the powers of darkness, were elevated to the position of secondary gods, to whom the regulation of the affairs of the fallen brethren was consigned but the consequences to the latter were terrible. The earth no longer yielded her abundance. Animals previously innocuous became vicious and destructive to life. Snakes became venomous and some plants poisonous. Man found out that he was naked and encumbering himself with clothing, lost the power of soaring through the air and skimming through the water, which in

> innocence he had possessed, and fierce strife raged between Bura and Tari, each contending for mastery.
>
> Out of this contest two great sects arose, one holding that Bura, the other that Tari had come off triumphant. The sect of Bura believed that Bura punished Tari by the curse on her sex, tantamount to the "in sorrow thou shalt bring forth children," and that Tari, however malevolent and destructive she may be, can only strike when Bura permits. The sect of Tari believe that their goddess cannot be frustrated by Bura in her evil designs, but if she can be persuaded by adoration to abstain from injuring, man will be free from misfortune. She alone therefore should be propitiated.
>
> Notwithstanding the tiff between Bura and Tari, their union was fruitful, and six godlings were produced to meet the primary wants of fallen man.
>
> First, Pidzu Pennu, the rain god; second, Burbhi Pennu, the goddess of spring, who gives new vegetation and first fruits; third, Pitteri Pennu, the god of increase and gain; fourth, Klambo Pennu, the god of the chase; fifth, Loha Pennu, the iron god or god of war; sixth, Sundi Pennu, the god of boundaries.

The biblical elements are so transparently evident in this legend that their derivative value is not to be doubted. The transition into some local pagan mythological traditions is also very obvious. Clearly then we must distinguish between what we call "parallels" and what is probably the legacy of Christian missionaries. (But cf. ibid., p. 113 on the possible influence of the Jews of China.)

So I shall not venture into this tricky and obstacle-strewn region of research,[6] but merely present a body of raw, untreated material, which may possibly best be analyzed in greater depth by others more competent than myself.

---

6. For a comprehensive description and analysis of the various views on this subject, see Stith Thompson, *The Folktale*, Berkeley, Los Angeles, London, 1946, part 4, pp. 367 et seq.

So to recap, this is merely a random collection, which, perhaps, may encourage others to examine the various examples in greater depth and detail. And if a sufficient number of individual studies be carried out, there may even emerge such cumulative conclusions. So this material is presented as merely the first step in a possible development process, which I gladly leave to others.[7]

Finally, I have added an Appendix of a somewhat technical nature, in which I discuss the phenomenon of Indian loanwords in Jewish sources, serving as an indication of the various types of cultural contacts between these two cultures.

---

7. See Tudor Parfitt, *The Lost Tribes of Israel: The History of a Myth*, Weidenfeld & Nicolson, London, 2002, pp. 132–148, for a fascinating survey of the views on the relationship of Indians to Jews.

Part I

Biblical Parallels

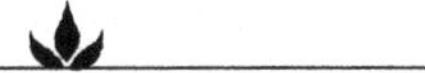

1. Macrocosm and Micocosm in Creation[8]

Tractate *Avot* of the Mishna is a repository of ethical teachings. *Avot of R. Nathan* is a parallel collection or alternate collection. A passage devoted to the creation of the world runs thus:

> R. Yosi ha-Galili says, "Whatever the Holy One, blessed be He, created[9] on earth, He created also in man. To what may the matter be compared? To some who took a piece of wood and wanted to make many forms on it but had no room to make them, so he was distressed. But someone who draws forms on the earth can go on drawing and can spread them out as far as he likes.
>
> But the Holy One, blessed be He, may His great name be blessed and ever, in His wisdom and understanding created the whole of the world, He created the heaven and the earth, above

8. I discussed this in greater detail in Appendix V of my article entitled "Jerusalem Axis Mundi," which appeared in *the Joshua Schwartz Volume, Journal for the Land of Israel Studies and Archeology*, vol. 12–13, 2020, pp. 159[x]-242[x].

9. On Indian aboriginal creation myths, see Verrier Elwin, *Myths of Middle India*, Madras, 1949, chapter 1, pp. 3 et seq. Note on p. 38 that according to the Gond myth of Patangarh, Mandla District, "At the beginning there was nothing but water,", and cf. *Genesis* 1:1, and cf. ibid., p. 43, on the "world above the waters of the Under World," and see *Genesis* ibid., verse 6. But on analysis, these may not be real parallels.

and below, and created in man whatever He created in His world.

In the world He created forests, and in man He created forests: the hairs on his head.

In the world He created wild beasts and in man He created wild beasts: lice.

In the world He created channels and in man He created channels: his ears.

Salt water in the world, salt water in man: his urine.

Streams in the world, streams in man: man's tears.

Walls in the world, walls in man: his lips.

Doors in the world, doors in man: his teeth.

Firmaments in the world, firmaments in man: his tongue.

Fresh water in the world, fresh water in man: his spit.

Stars in the world, stars in the man: his cheeks.

Towers in the world, towers in man: his neck.

[Goldin:] masts in the world, masts in man: his arms.

Pins in the world, pins in man: his fingers.

A King in the world, a King in man: his head [Goldin: heart].

Grapeclusters in the world, grapeclusters in man: his breasts.

Counselors in the world, counselors in man: his kidneys.

Millstones in the world, millstones in man: his intestines [which grind up food].

[Goldin:] mashing mills in the world, and mashing mills in man: the spleen.

Pits in the world, a pit in man: his belly button.

Flowing streams in the world and a flowing stream in man: his blood.

Trees in the world and trees in man: his bones.

Hills in the world and hills in man: his buttocks.

[Goldin:] pestle and mortar in the world and pestle and mortar in man: his joints.

Horses in the world and horses in man: his legs.

The angel of death in the world and the angel of death in man: his heels.

> Mountains and valleys in the world and mountains and valleys in man: when he is standing, he is like a mountain, when he is lying down, he is like a valley.
>
> Thus, you have learned that whatever the Holy One, blessed be He, created on earth, He created also in man."[10]

J. Neusner summarizes as follows (ibid., p. 190):

> The general theme of creation accounts for the inclusion of this catalogue, which also underlines the opening point: a human being is equivalent to the entire world. Accordingly, the associative principle of redaction blends exquisitely with the expository one, since the theme and the point the redactor wished to make from the start to the finish now join together, the mark of a stunning piece of redaction.

As to [Goldin] masts, the Hebrew has סתידראות, to which Schechter (ibid., note 32) gives a variant סרדיוטות. Krauss, in his pioneering *Lehnwörter,*[11] equated this with סרדיוט, on the basis of Schechter's variant.[12] But the variant was more likely a copyist's mistaken attempt to tease out a reasonable reading. Such a reading is difficult to justify contextually, as Goldin's "masts" gives no clear etymology. I would suggest a probable corruption from Greek *stauloeidēs,* cross-like, i.e., the yard-arm of a ship, which suits the notion of a man's arm.[13]

And concerning (Goldin) mashing mills, he probably based this interpretation on Schechter's suggested emendation (note 23), ממסים. But this has no textual basis and is most unlikely. Julius Preuss rejected previous suggestions, explaining that:

10. J. Neusner's translation (with slight changes) from his *The Fathers According to Rabbi Natan: An Analytical Translation and Explanation*, Atlanta, GA, 1986, pp. 189–190.

11. S. Krauss, *Grechische und Lateinische Lehnwörter in Talmud, Midrash und Targum,* vol. 2, Berlin, 1899, p. 414b, s.v. סתידראות.

12. Ibid., p. 413ab, s.v. סרדיוט.

13. See my *Nautica Talmudica,* Ramat-Gan and Leiden, 1986, p. 41.

> The meaning is "soft and liquefied", just like the consistency of the spleen. Similarly, Galen calls the spleen *chaunos* meaning loose or spongy [from נמס, to melt, D. S.].[14]

This too is not wholly persuasive. I would, therefore, tentatively suggest an etymology for the Greek *onommos e katharas* meaning cleanser, as the spleen cleanses the blood.[15]

The whole *Avot de-R. Natan* passage is a classical exposition by R. Yosi ha-Galili of the concept of the human body being a sort of parallel microcosm to the macrocosm of the universe. Thus, he opens his lists of comparisons:

> But the Holy One blessed be He, may His name be blessed for an eternity, in His wisdom and sagacity created the whole world, the heaven and the earth, the celestial regions and the lower regions, and He created in Man all that He created in His world...

There then follow some twenty-eight examples of these parallelisms (see above). In a reverse fashion we read in the Indian *Purusa Sūkta*, the *Hymn of the Cosmic Man*:

> ... From his (Purusa's) navel was produced the air; from his head the sky was evolved; from his feet the earth; from his ear the quarters, thus they fashioned the worlds.[16]

For a similar notion of the macrocosmic being out of which the world was created see Verrier Elwin, *Myths of Middle India*, Oxford

14. Julius Preuss, *Biblical and Talmudic Medicine* (transl. and ed. by Fred Rosner), New York, 1973, p. 99.

15. *Greek Dictionary* p.1177a, s.v. *onommos e katharas*.

16. *Purusa Sukta, Hymn of the Cosmic Man* (Rig Veda 10:90, verse 3), transl. A. A. Macdonell, *A Vedic Reader for Students*, Madras, 1951.

University Press 1969, pp. 9–10, and indeed the whole chapter on creation, ibid., pp. 3–50.

We may also find an expansion of this theme of "correspondences" in Muslim Sufi mysticism, in the sense of "spiritual" correspondence:

> Ibn Arabi (1165–1240) describes the setting out of the universe through correspondences which relate the macrocosm to the microcosm: "God set the sun to be a lamp to give light to the people of the earth (71:15–16), and likewise He has set the Spirit (*rūh*) in the body to give light to the body thereby, so that when it departs at death, the body is darkened, just as the earth is darkened when the sun disappears. Then He set the intellect (*ʿaql*) to be as the moon which shines in the heavenly vault, at one time waxing and at another waning. At its beginning it is small, being the new moon, just as the moon increases to the light of its fullness, after which it begins to decrease… Then He placed in the sky the five stars (Mercury, Venus, Jupiter, Mars and Saturn), namely, the stars of retrograde motion which run backwards, to which correspond the five senses, i.e. taste, smell, touch, hearing and seeing.
>
> Then in the world of the heavens He set a Throne and a Pedestal. [Cf. *Isaiah* 66:1 … 'The heaven is my throne, and the earth my footstool' = pedestal. D. S.] The Throne He brought into existence and set as something to which the hearts of His servants might turn, a place to which they might raise their hands, not as a place where He Himself might be or as a symbol of His Qualities, for in the case of the Merciful One-exalted be He – the sitting is but one of the qualifying, descriptive epithets which are connected with His essence, whereas the Throne is one of the things He created. It is not attached to Him, does not touch Him. He is not borne by it, and He has no need of it. As for the Pedestal, it is the storehouse of His secrets, the quiver for holding His lights; and the heavens and the earth are the depository for all that is in the circle of His wide-spreading Pedestal. So He has set man's breast to be as the Pedestal, for in

> it are stored all the attainments of knowledge. It stands like a courtyard at the gate of the heart and the soul, with two doors opening to them so that all good proceeding from the heart or evil proceeding from the soul is stored in the breast from which it proceeds to the productive members.
>
> The heart He set to be as the Throne. His Throne in the heavens is something known about, whereas His throne on earth is a lodging-place, and thus the throne of the heart is a nobler thing than the Throne of the heavens, for that Throne is not wide enough for Him; does not bear Him; does not perceive Him; but this throne is something towards which at all times He looks, to which He reveals Himself, or to which He sends down from heaven His bounty, for He has said: 'My heavens were not wide enough to hold Me, nor My earth,' [Cf. *1 Kings* 8:27:... 'Behold, the heaven and the heaven heavens cannot contain Thee,' and also *2 Chronicles* 6:18. – D. S.] but the heart of my believing servant holds Me'".[17]

And as a further expansion of the discussion of this field we find an interesting parallel in the thirteenth-century Ebstorf map. It represents the world as the body of Christ, with Christ's head situated at the head of the map next to Paradise, his feet in the west, and his hands gathering in the north and the south. Already mentioned above, Jerusalem, as the navel of the world, is at the center.[18]

Harvey suggests that the T-O map may also be seen as a symbol of the Passion of Christ.[19] He suggests that the T in the T-O Schemata

---

17. Ibn 'Arabi, *Shaarat-al-kawn*, transl. Arthur Jeffery, *Journal of Royal Asiatic Society* 1959, pp. 119–121. Also see Laleh Bakhtiar, *Sufi: Expressions of the Mystic Quest*, London, 1976, p. 118. Further examples of the "Earth-Body" correspondence are found in David Maclagan, *Creation Myths: Man's Introduction to the World*, London, 1977, pp. 25–27, 90.

18. See Harvey apud J. B. Harley and David Woodward, ibid., p. 291, figs. 18.2, 18.3, and p. 310.

19. Ibid., p. 334. On T-O maps, see what I wrote in my article "Jerusalem: Axis Mundi," apus *The Joshua Schwartz Volume: Jerusalem and Eretz Israel: A Journal for Land*

represents a cross, but of the *tau* variety (the *crux commissa*). This is particularly noticeable when the ends of the crossbar are angled or truncated.[20] Furthermore, when the body of Christ is superimposed on the map of the earth in an all-embracing dying gesture, as in the aforementioned Ebstorf map, the map itself becomes a clear symbol of the salvation of the world. He further points out that even the twenty-four monstrous races are embraced by the arms of Christ, although symbolically they are by his left hand at the very extremity of the world.

But here we have gone far beyond the parameters of this study.

of Israel Studies and Archeology, eds. Eyal Baruch and Avraham Faust, 12–13, 2020, pp. 203^{x}–207^{xx}. P. D. A. Harvey, "Medieval *Mappaemundi*," apud *A History of Cartography*, vol. 1, *Cartography in Prehistoric, Ancient, and Medieval Europe and the Mediterranean*, eds. J. B. Harley and David Woodward, Chicago and London 1987, pp. 296–297.

20. Referring to Jonathan T. Lanman, in *Cartographica* 18/4, 1981, pp. 18–22, and Harley's fig. 18.37.

2. The Diminishing of the Moon

In *Genesis* 1:16 we read, "And God made the two great lights – namely the sun and the moon: the greater light to rule the day and the lesser light to rule the night; and the stars." On this verse the Talmud in *B. Hullin* 60b relates in the name of R. Shimon ben Pazi as follows:

> It is written "and God made the two great lights", … and it is written "the greater light… and the lesser light." The moon said to the Lord, "Can two Kings use one crown?" He replied, "Go and diminish yourself."… etc. Cf. *B. Shavuot* 9a.

See L. Ginzberg, *The Legends of the Jews*, vol. 1, Philadelphia, 1909, pp. 23–24, and vol. 5, Philadelphia, 1925, pp. 34–37, for full references to this motif.

In Robert Briffault's *The Mothers*, vol. 2, New York, 1927, p. 580, I found the following:

> The Garros of Assam say that, "The moon was the brighter and more beautiful of the two, and exited the envy and resentment of her brother. The Metheis say that there were once two sons, but they quarreled and the wounded became pale… Thus in Brahmanic literature it is stated that the sun "took to himself the moon's shine; although the two are similar, the moon shines much less, for its shine has been taken away from it." (See A.

> Playfair, *The Garos*, p. 85; *Satapatha Brāhmana* 11:9, 4, 3; *The Sacred Books of the East*, vol. 1, p. 37.)

Briffault there notes the parallel with rabbinic sources, and continues to show partial parallels in Islamic literature.

It is of interest to note that in Hebrew the moon can be masculine *yareah* (frequently found in the Scriptures), or feminine *levanah* (meaning "the white one"), *Isaiah* 24:23; 30:26, *Canticles* 6:10. Likewise, the sun is both masculine, *Shemesh*, and feminine *Hamah*. Briffault (ibid., pp. 595–596) states that:

> In Indian mythology the moon is a god, not a goddess. The moon is a male among the Nagas, the Todas, the Khasis, the Shans, the Siamese.

He also shows that in other areas the moon is feminine (ibid., p. 594). But he is not correct in stating (p. 596) that "in all Semitic languages the moon is masculine and the sun feminine". However, in vol. 3, pp. 46–47, he shows that "the sexes of the heavenly bodies commonly become reversed…", explaining that "the 'bisexual' character of primitive deities is not the expression of a transcendental conception of metaphysical hermaphroditism, but a natural result of the combination of male attributes and feminine interests in the primitive lunar deity and of the facile inconsistency of primitive thought and tradition". I am not sure if this is the explanation for the different terms used in the Hebrew language. See also ibid., pp. 76 et seq.

3. The Footstool of God

In *Isaiah* 66:1, we read: "The heaven is my throne and the earth my footstool (or pedestal)." Ibn Arabi (1165–1240) elaborates on this theme:

> There in the world of the heavens He set a Throne and a Pedestal... His Throne in the heavens is something known about, whereas His throne on earth is a lodging-place, and thus the throne of the heart is a nobler thing than the Throne of the heavens, for that Throne is not wide enough for Him; does not bear Him; does not perceive Him; but this throne is something towards which at all times He looks, to which He reveals Himself, or to which He sends down from heaven His bounty, for He has said: "My heavens were not wide enough to hold Me, nor My earth, [Cf. *1 Kings* 8:27:... 'Behold, the heaven and the heaven heavens cannot contain Thee,' and also *2 Chronicles* 6:18. D. S.] but the heart of my believing servant holds Me". (Ibn 'Arabi, *Shaarat-al-kawn*, transl. Arthur Jeffery, *Journal of Royal Asiatic Society* 1959, pp. 119–121.)[21]
>
> See R. V. Russell and Mira Lal, *The Tribes and Castes on the Central Provinces of India*, London, 1916, vol. 2, p. 327: It is said that Bhunjia women are never allowed to sit either on a footstool or a bed-cot, because these are considered to be seats of the deities.

21. See Laleh Bakhtiar, *Sufi: Expressions of the Mystic Quest*, London, 1976, p. 118.

4. Creation of Adam as an Androgynous and His "Separation"

The Midrash in *Genesis Rabba* 8:1, ed. Theodor Albeck, vol. 1, p. 55, on the verse in *Genesis* 1:26, seeks to relate this verse to that which we read in *Psalms* 139:5, "Thou hast beset – *tzaratani* – behind and before." *Tzaratani* is interpreted homiletically as if it were from the root *tzur*, form, coming to mean "You have formed one behind and in front." Thus, R. Shmuel ben Nachman (Eretz Yisrael c. 250–320 C.E.) says:

> When the Holy One blessed be He created the first Man– i.e. Adam -, he formed him double-faced) *diprosopon* = Greek διπρόσωπον) – and he sawed him [apart] and made a back (*gabayim*) this way and a back this way.[22]

While R. Yirmiyah ben E[lear] (Eretz Yisrael c. 290–320 C.E.) states (ibid.) that Adam was created androgynous, double-sexed, meaning that the sexes had to be separated. These authorities interpret *Genesis* 2:21, "and He took one of his *tzalotav*" – usually translated as ribs,

22. See Moshe Idel, *Kabbalah and Eros*, New Haven and London, 2005, chapter 2, "*Du-Partzufin*: Interpretations of Androgyneity in Jewish Mysticism," pp. 53–103, 268–281; idem, "Androgyny and Equality in the Thosophico–Theurgical Kabbalah," *Diogenes* 52 (4), 2005, pp. 27–38; Pinchas Giller, "Nesirah: Myth and Androgyny in Late Kabbalistic Practice," *Journal of Jewish Thought and Philosophy* 12/3, 2003, pp. 63–86, etc.

but here interpreted as "sides" (referring to *Exodus* 26:20: *u-le-tzela ha-mishkan* – and the *side* of the tabernacle).

The editors of *Genesis Rabba* (ibid., note to line 3) rightly point out that Freudenthal, in his *Hellenistische Studies*, vol. 1, p. 69, found parallels to this notion of separating the two parts of the first human being into masculine and feminine entities in the works of Plato (*Symposium* 189d) and Philo (*De. M. Opif.* 24.46, etc.). So also M. Sachs, in his *Baiträge*, vol. 1, Berlin, 1852, p. 57, and Louis Ginzberg, in his *The Legends of the Jews*, vol. 5, Philadelphia, 1925, note 42, with additional references and a detailed discussion. But what for us is of special interest is what we find in the *Brihadaranyaka Upanisad* 1:4.3, in Swami Nikhilananda's translation (in *The Upanishads*, vol. 3, New York, 1956), p. 115:

> He [namely Viraj] was not at all happy. Therefore a person [even today] is not happy when alone. He desired a mate. He became the size of a man and wife in close embrace. He divided his body into two. From that [division] arose husband [*pati*] and wife [*patni*]. Therefore, as Yājnavalkya [one of the Vedic *rishis*] said, the body [before one accepts a wife] is one half of oneself, like the half of a split pea. Therefore this space is indeed filled by the wife. He was united with her. From that [union] human beings were born.[23]

---

23. See *In the Image of Man: The Indian Perception of the Universe through 2000 Years of Painting and Sculpture*, London, 1982, p. 216:

THE LORD WHO IS HALF WOMAN

The Lord who, though he stands in that sole sovereignty
which holds many rewards for his devotees,
himself wears only an animal-skin
Who, though his body is conjoined with that of his beloved,
is yet superior to ascetics whose minds are free
from material desires
Who, though he supports the whole world in his eight forms,
is yet not proud
May he lead you from the path of darkness,
that you see the way of goodness.

This benedictory verse of the god Shiva was written by the Sanskrit poet and playwright, Kālidāsa, in the 5th century AD as a prologue to one of his dramas. The "eight forms" referred to are explained by the commentator, Katyavema, as meaning the five elements – earth, water, fire, air and space – mentioned in connection with the *linga,* plus the visible symbols of time, the sun and moon, and the god's devotee himself, who is the eighth form of Shiva. The second line might appear to suggest that the god is imagined as joined in sexual intercourse with his consort, Pārvatī; but actually he is never represented thus. The poet is referring to a particular image of the god, which was iconographically established two or three centuries before Kālidāsa, representing the god in androgynous form. Sculptures representing this conception of Shiva are divided into male and female halves, the left half - always symbolically female - appearing as the goddess Pārvatī, the right half as the god himself. Great artistic skill is evident in many such sculptures, for only a master could integrate the male and female halves into an aesthetically convincing and pleasing whole.

In origin, this image derives from the concept of the hermaphroditic act of creation by a single creator. See the *Matsya Purāṇa* 3:1–2. 30–47, as found in Comelia Dimmitt and J. A. B. van Buiteen, *Classical Hindu Mythology: A Reader in the Sanskrit Purāṇas*, Philadelphia, 1978, p. 34:

> Now I shall relate what sprang from the body of Prajapati without benefit of mothers... then, clearing his pure body in two, the universal creator put the goddess Sāvitri in his heart in order to create the world. One half of himself he made into a woman's body, and the other half into a man. The woman he called Śatarūpā, and celebrated her as Sarasvati, Gāyatri and Brahmāṇi, O enemy burner. And so he made the goddess out of himself, from his own body....

And cf. ibid., p. 153.

> Mythologists of the Vishnu cult introduced a goddess as the personification of that god's trance-like sleep upon the waters at the instant of creation. The introduction of a female principle became necessary to lend credibility to the creation myth, though it was for as long as possible subordinated to the idea of an exclusively male creative power. Although in the androgynous images the female half is of equal physical statue, to the male half, the name of these icons suggests that we are looking at the god Shiva, whose generative force, when he assumes the role of universal creator, requires a female presence. In fact, the name of the image is Ardhanārīshvara, which means "The Lord Who is Half Woman" – a masculine concept which incorporates a female aspect, not a male-female partnership. This is borne out by another verse of Kālidāsa, in which the poet again invokes Shiva in his androgynous form:
>
> *Homage to the father-and-mother of the world,*
> *to him whose left half is his wife –*

This text describes how Viraj, later called Manu, after he had divided himself, was united with the woman Satarupa, his daughter, who now was his wife, and that from that union human beings were born (ibid., p. 110).[24]

Furthermore, the notion that for every man there is an ideal wife who will, as it were, complement him and thus complete and fulfill the ideal union is expressed in the Talmud in *B. Sotah* 2a, and *B. Sanhedrin* 22a, in the name of Rav Yehudah in the name of Rav (died Babylon 249 C.E.) in the dictum:

Whose left eye shrinks from the mere glance of the right.

> These sculptures are not fanciful depictions of the ideal couple wedded together in matrimony; that is represented in other, more conventional tableaux. The Ardhanarīshvara image is indisputably bisexual in appearance, but the cosmogenetic concept which it expresses is essentially and dominantly masculine.

For a beautiful picture of *Shiva Ardhanarishvara* from the Mankot workshop of circa 1715, see B. N. Goswarny and Caron Smith, *Domains of Wonder: Selected Masterworks of Indian Painting*, San Diego Museum of Art, 2006, p. 197, no. 80. The authors add the following commentary to the picture (p. 196):

> In the making of an image of *Ardhanarishvara*, the painter or the sculptor almost always has to rise to a challenge. The conception is extraordinary, not only at the physical or visual level, but also in the metaphysical sense. *Ardhanarishvara* – literally, "half woman, half Lord," or "The Lord whose half is woman" – is more than an androgynous form, for it is many things and many ideas: a biune coming together of the active and the passive principle, of *purusha* and *prakriti*, complete wholeness in equal parts. In visual terms, it is always Shiva, the great reclusive god, and his consort Parvati, who are rendered conjoined, not fused together: the left half is the female and therefore: Parvati; the right half of Shiva, the male.

On the Master of Mankot and his work, see B. N. Goswami and Eberhard Fisher, *Pahari Masters: Court Painters of Northern India*, Zurich, 1992, pp. 95–125.

See also T. Richard Blurton, *Hindu Art*, Cambridge, MA, 1993, p. 96, fig. 57, where the river Ganges is flowing from the dreadlocks of Shiva, while Parvati is crowned, and carries the trident and drum, while she carries a rosary (Rajasthan late eighteenth – early nineteenth century).

24. This parallel was noted by David Mevorach Seidenberg, in his *Kabbalah and Ecology: God's Image in the More Than Human World*, Cambridge, England, 2015, p. 246, note 792. See also Joseph Campbell, *The Masks of God: Oriental Mythology*, 1962, pp. 9–13.

> Forty days before the formation of the embryo a voice from heaven (*bat-kol*) goes forth and announces, "the daughter of So and So is for So and So..."

And this seems also to be indicated in *Tikkunei ha-Zohar: Tikkun 58*. Admittedly, says the Talmud, this does not always work out as "announced," and, in that case, there may be a second partnership (*zivug sheni*). But the similarities between the Hindu myth and the midrashic tradition are surely tantalizing.[25]

25. See further Krishna Sivaraman, "The Mysticism of Male-Female Relationships," *Sexual Archetypes, East and West*, ed. Bina Gupta, New York, 1987, p. 93. See further, Adiel Schremer, *Male and Female He Created Them*, Jerusalem, 2003 (Hebrew).

Incidentally, see Ginzberg, ibid., p. 72, note 15, on Jewish sources describing the elements out of which Adam was created, and compare the Slavonic Christian traditions of this theme in Alexander Kulik and Sergey Minov, *Biblical Pseudepigrapha in Slavonic Tradition*, Oxford, 2016, pp. 44, 54–56. But here we have strayed far afield.

See further J. G. Frazer, *Folk-Lore in the Old Testament*, vol. 1, London, 1918, pp. 17–22.

5. Creation of Man and the Fall

The creation of humankind in world mythology has been the subject of considerable research, and numerous versions of this theme have been collected. The biblical narrative is, of course, well-known from *Genesis* 1:26–28, 2:18–22. However, I was surprised to find a Lepcha version in Yishey Doma's *Legends of the Lepchas: Folk Tales from Sikkim*, New Delhi, 2010, p. 1–3:

> In the beginning, when there was nothing but vast emptiness on earth and in the sky, Itbu-moo, Mother Creator, set out to execute a great plan. She first shaped Kongchen Kongchlo, his wives, Samo Gayzong and Paki Chyu, his brothers, Pawo Hungree and Bagok Chyu, and other mountains of *chyu bee*. As complements to the mountains she created *daa*, the lakes and *roong*, the rivers.
>
> She thought she was done, but something appeared to be missing. She surveyed her handiwork. Why did her creation feel empty? Taking a ball of fresh snow from the summit of Kongchen Kongchlo, Itbu-moo created the first man, Fudongthing, the most-powerful one.[26] Mother Creator remained unsatisfied. She decided to give Fudongthing, her pet creation, a companion. So she took a bit of *a-yong* [marrow] from Fudongthing's bones

26. Since Sikkim is in Trans Himalayas, snow is the material from which man is created, as opposed to earth from the biblical area.

> and created the first woman, Nazong Nyu, the ever-fortunate one, as his sister. Later, both became chief deities of the Rongs or Lepchas.

There then follows the story of the Fall (cf. *Genesis*):

> Having created the first man and first woman, brother and sister, Itbu-moo called them and said, "You are the most beloved of all my creations. I have blessed both of you with supernatural powers. But both of you should live separately as true brother and sister. You can never live together." Both promised they would follow her decree. She then sent Fudongthing to live on top of a mountain called Nareng-Nangsheng Chyu and Nazong Nyu to Naho-Nathor Daa, a lake located just below the mountain. Itbu-moo also warned them that if they disobeyed her, she would not hesitate to send them down to the foothills to live in the realm of misery.
>
> Fudongthing and Nazong Nyu lived happily enough for some time but one thought began to plague their minds – they were living solitary lives. Nazong Nyu had grown up into a beautiful young woman. She felt life without anyone to share it with was terribly lonely and monotonous. As there was no one else, she thought a lot about Fudongthing, who had grown up into a handsome man. But she remembered ltbu-moo's warning and kept away from him.
>
> Everything was well with their world. As long as Fudongthing and Nazong Nyu behaved in a manner befitting their celestial lineage, they prospered and never suffered any real grief. Their lives in the territory of the gods were filled with happiness.
>
> But they were not content with happiness alone. And like all humans, they were capable of both good and evil. They were soon tired of following the dictates of Mother Creator. Failing to resist temptation, Nazong Nyu constructed a golden ladder and climbed up Nareng-Nangsheng Chyu to meet Fudongthing.
>
> Fudongthing too did not pay heed to Itbu-moo's warning.

They began to secretly meet at Tarkol-Partam, a flat piece of meadowland between the mountain and the lake.

One day they decided to meet at Sugyum Sugbling, another lake near Naho-Nathor Daa. Nazong Nyu removed her bangle and kept it near her pillow, as she found it uncomfortable while sleeping. The bangle fell into the lake and from there sprouted *suneol kung*, a mountain palm tree, which later became the abode of Lasso Mung Puno, demon king.

So absorbed were Fudongthing and Nazong Nyu in their own company that they forgot Itbu-moo and her divine decree and started living together. As a result of this forbidden union, soon a monster-child was born to them. On the birth of the child they remembered ltbu-moo's decree. Both were afraid that Mother Creator would come to know what mischief they had been up to. "This is an unholy child. We cannot keep him under our roof," said Fudongthing and threw the child away in the forest. Year after year, a monster-child was born to the couple. And each time they threw the baby away – they would simply leave the babies in cliffs, crags or caves. In this way, seven children were lost.

6. The Flood Story

R. V. Russell, *The Tribes and Castes of the Central Provinces of India*, 1916, vol. 3, pp. 326–327, sect. *Kamār*, writes as follows:

> They tell a curious story about the origin of the world, which recalls that of the Flood. They say that in the beginning God created a man and a woman to whom two children of opposite sex were born in their old age. Mahādeo, however, sent a deluge over the world in order to drown a jackal who had angered him. The old couple heard that there was going to be a deluge, so they shut up their children in a hollow piece of wood with provision of food to last them until it should subside. They then closed up the trunk, and the deluge came and lasted for twelve years, the old couple and all other living things on the earth being drowned, but the trunk floated on the face of the waters. After twelve years Mahādeo created two birds and sent them to see whether his enemy the jackal had been drowned. The birds flew over all the corners of the world, but saw nothing except a log of wood floating on the surface of the water, on which they perched. After a short time they heard low and feeble voices coming from inside the log. They heard the children saying to each other that they only had provision for three days left. So the birds flew away and told Mahādeo, who then caused the flood to subside, and taking out the children from the log of

> wood, heard their story. He thereupon brought them up, and they were married, and Mahadeo gave the name of a different caste to every child who was born to them, and from them all the inhabitants of the world are descended.

The similarities to the biblical Flood story in *Genesis* 6:13–22, are obvious, even to the motif of the birds. The theme of the deluge was treated exhaustively by Theodor H. Gaster, *Myth, Legend, and Custom in the Old Testament: A Comparative Study with Chapters from Sir James G. Frazer's "Folklore in the Old Testament,"* Harper Torchbook, 1975, in vol. 1, pp. 82–138, with a special section on India (pp. 94–97), noting the *Kamār* story and with a full bibliography, pp. 352–353. See also the brief but very clear and cogent remarks in Lewis Spence's masterful booklet *The Outline of Mythology*, New York, 1961, pp. 76–79.

A somewhat different flood story is to be found in George Kotturan, *Folk Tales of Sikkim*, New Delhi, 1976, chapter 8, pp. 42–44, where a pigeon brings the message of hope that the flood will subside. See also Frazer, ibid., pp. 183–234.

Yet another flood story is brought by J. R. Subba, in his *History, Culture and Customs of Sikkim*, New Delhi, 2008, pp. 201–202 [the grammatical errors appear in the original text – D. S.]:

> **The Great Deluge:** The Almighty Goddess *Tagera Ningwaphuma* found that the world was filled with sins. The human being whom She thought to be Her greatest creation were committing all kinds of sins for their selfish ends. There were only a couple named *Sodhung Lepmuhang* (Demi-God) and *Laoti Phungphahangma* (Demi-Goddess) who were trying to bring people to the path of virtue and goodness but they could not succeed. The Goddess knew this, so She decided to save these couple only by destroying all others.
>
> The Almighty Goddess sent a messenger *Musekha Sekhanama* to *Sodhung Lepmuhang* in the form of a small fish of a stream. One day *Sodhung Lepmuhang* rose early and went to bathe in

a nearby stream. There, he found a small fish that asked him to help by transferring him to a pond as a big fish was trying to swallow her. The fish also told him that he would save him from distress for this good act. *Sodhung Lepmuhang* picked her and put the fish into a pond. After sometime as he was passing by the pond he heard the voice of the same fish that requested him to take her to a river as he was growing fast and the pond would be too small for her, she was put into the river.

Days rolled by, *Sodhung Lepmuhang* had forgotten the fish and the work he did for her. One day as he was passing by the river, he heard the voice of the same fish that had grown very big. The fish again asked to put her into the sea as she was fast growing in size and the river would be too small for him. The fish further told him that she would come back to help him in a great deluge which is likely to come and destroy all men of the earth. She further instructed *Sodhung Lepmuhang* to build a big ship of many compartments where pair of animals, birds and other creatures should be kept. The food also should be collected and kept in the ship. The fish further told him that as all the earth would go down the water she should come near the ship along with his wife *Laoti Phungphahangma.* She would have a long horn where he should tie the top of the ship with a strong knot. The ship would not sink but would follow her. *Sodhung Lepmuhang* heard the words of the fish and believed each word uttered by the fish.

Sodhung Lepmuhang returned home and did everything as desired by the fish. A big ship was built having many compartments where pair of each animal, bird and other creatures were taken into the ship. The stock of food was also deposited inside the ship. He then along with his wife shut the door of the ship.

Soon after torrential rain started coming down from the sky. There was darkness everywhere. The deluge started enveloping on earth. Nothing could survive in the deluge. At that time a fish of huge size appeared near the ship and *Sodhung Lepmuhang* tied the ship to the horn of the huge fish. The ship went after the fish.

> After days and nights the rains stopped and there was silence everywhere. The sun appeared in the sky. The water started going down. The hills around started appearing. The ship stopped on a hillock. The fish told *Sodhung Lepmuhang* to go down to the earth with all the creatures of the ship to start a new life of peace and happiness and also guide the future generation, the path of sustainable peace and happiness. For this, the Limboo Kiratas invoke *Sodhung Lepmuhang* as Demi-God even today for all social and religious rituals.
>
> The folk tale is based on the myth of Mundhum of the Limboo Kiratha tribe. The Aryans too have a similar kind of legend of the deluge. The theme of the legend is the same. The Mundhum of the Kiratas has come down since generation from mouth to mouth. This legend of the Aryans is found written in the volume of Satpath Brahman which is supposed to be written five hundred years before the Christ. It may be assumed that the oral legend of the Kitara is older than that of the Aryans. It is also interesting to note that the legend of Noah's ark of the Bible has the same overarching theme. A deep study into the folk legends of Sikkim and its tribes would help relate all these legends.

Subba refers us to M. M. Gurung and R. P. Lama, *Sikkim Study Series – Culture*, vol. III, Govt. of Sikkim, 2004, pp. 71–72.

Finally we should recall what we read in the Matsya Purṇa 1:11–35. As found in Comelia Dimmitt and J. A. B. van Buitenen, *Classical Hindu Mythology: A Reader in the Sanskrit Purāna*, Philadelphia, 1978, pp. 72–73:

> Thus addressed by Madhusūdana, Manu asked him, "O blessed one, how soon will this intermediary dissolution occur? And how, O guardian, shall I protect the creatures? And when shall we meet again, you and I. O Madhusūdana?"
>
> "Beginning then," said the Fish, "there will be a drought on the surface of the earth lasting a full hundred years, and a brutal famine. Seven cruel rays of the sun will deal death to the weak,

and there will be seven times seventy solar rays the color of fiery coals. At the close of the Age the submarine fire will blaze forth, and burning poison will flow from the mouth of Saṃkarṣaṇa in the netherworld, and also from the third eye of Bhava. The three worlds, aflame, will crumble, great seer, and the entire earth will be burned to ashes. Space will be scorched by the heat, O enemy-burner, and the world with its gods and constellations will be utterly annihilated.

"Six rain clouds will bring destruction: Bhīmanāda (Awful Roar), Droṇa (Bucket), Caṇḍa (Cruel), Balāhaka (Thundercloud), Vidyutpatāka (Lightning Banner) and Śoṇa (Crimson). And as they flood the earth, clouds will form because of the fire, like sweat, and the turbulent oceans will merge together into a single sea. They will turn the entire triple world into one vast sheet of water.

"Then you must take the seeds of life from everywhere and load them into the boat of the Vedas. Fasten to it the rope I shall give you, O well-vowed one, and tie the boat to my horn. When even all the gods have been burned up. O enemy-burner, you alone shall survive, by my power, along with Soma, Sūrya. Brahmā and myself, and the four directions, the holy river Namadā, the great seer Mārkaṇḍeya, Bhava, the Vedas, the Purāṇas and all the sciences. All of these, along with yourself, shall be saved when that vast ocean is all that is left in the dissolution at the end of the Cākṣusa Manvantara. At the start of the next creation, which you shall rule, I shall again promulgate the Vedas, O lord of earth." So speaking, the lord vanished on the spot.

Manu resorted to Yoga, by the grace of Vāsudeva, until the flood began, as prophesied. When the aforementioned time came, as Vāsudeva had said. Janārdana appeared in the form of a horned fish and a serpent in the form of a rope approached Manu's side. The virtuous king collected all the creatures and loaded them into the boat by Yoga (i.e., through the use of yogic techniques). Then he fastened the boat to the fish's horn with

> the rope made of the snake. And prostrating himself before Janārdana, he stepped in the ship.

A different version of this legend may be found in Prof. Weber's edition of the *Satapatha Brāhmana*, as cited by Monier Williams in his *Indian Wisdom*, London, 1876, pp. 32–34:

> There lived in ancient time a holy man,
> Called Manu, who by penances and prayers
> Had won the favour of the lord of heaven.
> One day they brought him water for ablution;
> Then, as he washed his hands, a little fish
> Appeared and spoke in human accents thus–
> .... The fish replied, 'A flood will sweep away
> All creatures, I will rescue thee from that.'
> ...then he [the fish] spake again–
> 'In such and such a year the flood will come;
> There construct a ship and pay me homage.
> When the flood rises, enter thou the ship,
> And I will rescue thee.'...
> And in the very year the fish enjoined
> He built a ship and paid the fish respect,
> And there took refuge when the flood arose.
> Soon near him swam the fish, and to its horn
> Manu made fast the cable of his vessel.
> Thus drawn along the waters Manu passed
> Beyond the northern mountain. Then the fish,
> Addressing Manu, said, 'I have preserved thee;
> Quickly attach the ship to yonder tree.
> But, lest the waters sink from under thee;
> As fast as they subside, so fast shalt thou
> Descend the mountain gently after them.'
> Thus he descended from the northern mountain.
> The flood had swept away all living creatures;
> Manu alone was left...

Monier Williams comments (p. 34) that in the Mahābhārata the fish is the incarnation of Brahmā, who assumed that form in order to prevent the pious Manu from perishing in the flood.

We may further note that in the rabbinic legend:

> One animal, the reem, Noah could not take into the ark. On account of its huge size it could not find room therein. Noah therefore tied it to the ark, and it ran behind. Also he could not make space for the giant Og, the king of Bashan. He sat on top of the ark securely, and in this way escaped the flood of waters.... (Louis Ginzberg, *The Legends of the Jews*, vol. 1, Philadelphia, 1909, p. 160.)

See idem, vol. 4, Philadelphia, 1925, p. 181, notes 34 and 35, for sources.

7. Noah's Raven and Dove

In *Genesis* 8:6–12, as part of the Flood story, we read as follows:

> [6]And it came to pass at the end of forty days, that Noah opened the window of the ark which he had made. [7]And he sent forth a raven, which went forth to and fro, until the waters were dried up from off the earth. [8]And he sent forth a dove from him, to see if the waters were abated from off the face of the ground. [9]But the dove found no rest for the sole of her foot, and she returned unto him into the ark, for the waters were on the face of the whole earth; then he put forth his hand, and took her, and pulled her in unto him into the ark. [10]And he stayed yet other seven days; and again he sent forth the dove out of the ark. [11]And the dove came in to him in the evening; and lo in her mouth an olive-leaf freshly plucked; so Noah knew that the waters were abated from off the earth. [12]And he stayed yet other seven days; and sent forth the dove; and she returned not again unto him anymore.

Apparently this was not an uncommon use of birds in the East. They may be called "shore-sighting" birds. See *The Periplus of the Erythraean Sea*, transl. and annotated by Wilfred H. Schoff, New York… 1912, pp. 228–229, who writes as follows:

> Prof. T. W. Rhys Davids, in the *Journal of the Royal Asiatic*

Society 1899, p. 432, quotes an interesting Buddhist passage referring to early sea-trade as follows:

"In the Dialogues of the Buddha is a passage in the Kevaddha Sutta of Digha-5th cent B.C. The Buddha says:

"Long ago ocean-going merchants were wont to plunge forth upon the sea, on board a ship, taking with them a shore-sighting bird. When the ship was out of sight of land they would set the shoresighting bird free. And it would go to the East and to the South and to the West and to the North, and to the intermediate points, and rise aloft. If on the horizon it caught sight of land, thither it would go, but if not it would come back to the ship again. Just so brother," etc.

Cosmas Indicopleustes found this same custom in Ceylon in the 6th century A.D., merchants depending on shore-sighting birds instead of observations of the sun or stars.

There are similar passages in the oldest of the Vedas (see Gibson's *Rig Veda,* Vol. I):

"Varuna, who knows the path of the birds flying through the air, he, abiding in the ocean, knows also the course of ship."

"May Ushas dawn today, the excitress of chariots which are harnessed at her coming, as those who are desirous of wealth ships to sea."

"Do thou, Agni, whose countenance is turned to all sides, send off our adversaries, as if in a ship to the opposite shore. Do thou convey us in a ship across the sea for our welfare." (A remarkable prayer for safe conduct at sea.)

On Noah's dove see further Charles Pellat, *The Life and Works of Jahiz* (c. 776–869), transl. D. H. Hawks, Berkeley and Los Angeles, 1969, p. 149:

Noah's Dove

[III, 195] . . . the champion of pigeons says: Arabs, Bedouins and poets all agree that it was a dove that served as guide and scout to Noah; and it was that dove that asked God, as its reward [III,

196], for the necklace which its like wear around their necks. God granted it this privilege and vouchsafed it this adornment at Noah's instance, when the bird returned bearing a vine-shoot, its feet all covered with mud and clay; as recompense for the clay it received the privilege of having feet of a distinctive colour, and for its obedience and its reconnaissance work for Noah it received the necklace that adorns its neck.

Verses and discussions about the necklace are followed by more verses and a dissertation on the pedigree of pigeons.

8. The Tower of Babel

The story of the Tower of Babylon is well known to all from *Genesis* 11:1–9. However, interestingly enough a Lepcha legend bears some remarkable similarities: We shall quote in full, as it is recorded in Yishey Dama's *Legends of the Lepchas: Folktales for Sikkim*, New Delhi, 2018, pp. 47–49:

The Stairway to Heaven

A very long time ago, the Lepchas lived under the benign presence of Mount Khangchendzonga, [the third highest mountain in the Himalayas – D. S.] in the land where the sun shone all year round. Food was plentiful amidst the valleys and in the streams that flowed from the hills. Everyone led a contented, prosperous life.

One autumn morning, when the sky was blue and the sun was more brilliant than usual, a group of men had a sudden yearning to meet their Gods. So they put together a plan to go up to heaven, where they believed their Gods resided.

"Let us make a ladder to heaven and meet our Gods," said one of them and the idea pleased everyone.

Another said, "Let's make big earthen pots and put them one on top of the other to make a column. When the pillar of pots is high enough, we will climb it to reach the heavens and meet our Gods."

"That will be excellent!" – the others said. "How clever!"

And so they started looking for a suitable site. After days of travelling around the country, the men found a flat piece of land situated to the south of the river Romam in Daramdin in west Sikkim. They named this place Thallom Purtam or a flat land leading upwards.

Soon, all the potters in the land got busy. Some started shaping the clay into pots, others busied themselves collecting wood for lighting the fire in which to bake them, and the rest began the actual work of construction by piling the pots upside down, one over the other. The ladder to heaven went up, and up, and up. Oh, how proud the men were!

The stairway to heaven first rose above the roofs of the houses. Then it went above the treetops. It started to touch the clouds. When it almost touched the sky, the people climbing it could hardly hear each other speak. Some of the Lepcha men in the group, adept in making bamboo crafts and instruments, devised a *passongthop*.[27] When the string holding the instrument was pulled, it would make a certain noise, conveying a message over a considerable distance. They also invented the *blingthop*,[28] which was used to summon potters to work and to call them when the day's work was over.

When they were almost done, there was a serious breakdown of communication between the artisans working at the top and the ones at the bottom of the earthen-pot tower. The man right on top wanted to know how much further heaven was. So he asked for a hook. He looked down and shouted "*Kok vim yang ta* (Send up a hooked stick)." The message got passed along down the column. One worker, who could not hear properly asked, "What?" "*Kok* vim *yang ta*," repeated the man above him, but the other worker heard "*Cheyk ta* (Smash it down)."

Although the artisans at the top kept yelling, "*Kok vim yang*

27. A bamboo instrument split on both sides, held together with bamboo ropes.

28. A smaller version of the *passongthop*.

> *ta*," by the time the message got through to the bottom, it had become "*Chyek ta*."
>
> The workers below got very busy. They took their axes and began to hit the pots, smashing them to pieces. "What's happening?" called the men at the top. Then, there was a noise like thunder. The pots fell down upon each other and the men's aspiration to meet their Gods remained a dream.
>
> This is how the plains of Thallom Purtam came to be known as Ka Daa Raom Dyen (now called Daramdin), which means "We ourselves smashed it down".

This similarly was already noted by Theodor H. Gaster in his magnificent *Myth, Legend, and Custom in the Old Testament*, vol. 1, Glouchester, MA, 1975, p. 134 (sect. 49), referring us (p. 360, note 6a), to R. de Nebesky-Wajkowitz in *Anthropos* 48, pp. 889–897 and W. J. Muckcaus in Hastings' *Encyclopedia of Religion and Ethics*, New York, 1928, XI 511b, s.v. Sikkim.

A variant of this story is to be found in George Kotterran, *Folk Tales of Sikkim*, New Delhi, 1976, chapter 77, pp. 72–74, entitled "The Tower of Dharamdin." Here we may add as an interesting footnote that Stith Thompson, in his *Folk Tales of the North American Indians*, North Dighton, MA, 1995, p. 263 (no. XLV), has a Choctow version of The Tower of Babel (from D. Bushnell, *Bulletin of the Bureau of American Ethnology* XLVIII, 70), and cf. ibid., p. 360, note 307. Here we should also add Mircea Eliade's comments in his *Shamanism: Archaic Techniques of Ecstasy*, Princeton, 1964, pp. 487–494, section entitled "The Ladder – the Road of the Dead – Ascension."

In this context it is interesting to compare this theme with the parable attributed to the great Hassidic Master, R. Yisrael Baal Shem (1700–1760), as related by Martin Buber in his *Tales of the Hasidim*, New York, 1975, Book 1, pp. 54–55:

> Once the Baal Shem stood in the House of Prayer and prayed for a very long time. All his disciples had finished praying,

but he continued without paying any attention to them. They waited for him a good while, and then they went home. After several hours when they had attended to their various duties, they returned to the House of Prayer and found him still deep in prayer. Later he said to them: "By going away and leaving me alone, you dealt me a painful separation. I shall tell you a parable.

You know that there are birds of passage who fly to warm countries in the autumn. Well, the people in one of those lands once saw a glorious many-colored bird in the midst of a flock which was journeying through the sky. The eyes of man had never seen a bird so beautiful. He alighted in the top of the tallest tree and nested in the leaves. When the king of the country heard of it, he bade them fetch down the bird with his nest. He ordered a number of men to make a ladder up the tree. One was to stand on the other's shoulders until it was possible to reach up high enough to take the nest. It took a long time to build this living ladder. Those who stood nearest the ground lost patience, shook themselves free, and everything collapsed."

9. Looking Back: The Lot Story

Russell, ibid., vol. 4, p. 372, section on *Parja* caste:

In Bastar the caste are also known as Dhurwa, which may be derived from Dhur, the name applied to the body of Gonds as opposed to the Rāj-Gonds. In Bastar, Dhurwa now conveys the sense of a headman of a village. The tribe have three divisions, Thakara of Tagara, Peng and Mudara, of which only the first is found in Bastar. Thakara appears to be a corruption of Thākur, a lord, and the two names point to the conclusion that the Parjas were formerly dominant in this tract. They themselves have a story, somewhat resembling the one quoted above from Madras, to the effect that their ancestor was the elder brother of the first Rāja of Bastar when he lived in Madras, to the south of Warangal. From there he had to flee on account of an invasion of the Muhammadans, and was accompanied by the goddess Danteshwari, the tutelary deity of the Rājas of Bastar. At Bhadrachallam they met the Bhatras, and further on the Halbas. The goddess followed them, guiding their steps, but she strictly enjoined on the Rāja not to look behind him so as to see her. But when they came to the sands of the rivers Sankani and Dankani, the tinkle of the anklets of the goddess could not be heard for the sand. The Raja therefore looked behind him

> to see if she was following, on which she said that she could go no more with him, but he was to march as far as he could and then settle down. The two brothers settled in Bastar, where the descendants of the younger became the ruling clan, and those of the elder were their servants, the Parjas....

The theme of not looking back to see what is behind is, of course, familiar from the story of Lot's wife in *Genesis* 19:26, though Lot's wife came to a much less happy end when she turned into a pillar of salt, whereas Raja's descendants merely became the servants of the younger brother's descendants.

The taboo against looking back has been noted by Theodor H. Gaster in his *Myth, Legend, and Custom in the Old Testament*, vol. 1, 1975, pp. 159–160, with notes on pp. 365–366 (and cf. pp. 160–161, 366), where he brings a wealth of parallels to this motif, including the well-known one that Orpheus was not permitted to look back when he led Eurydice out of Hades (Ovid, *Met.* 10:1–77; Vergil, *Georgia* 4.489f.).

We may further compare the above to the legend recorded by W. Crooke in his *The Popular Religion and Folk-Lore of Northern India*, vol. 1, London, 1896, pp. 120–121:

> General Sleeman gives the legend of Dûlha Deo in another form.
>
> In descending into the valley of the Narmadâ, over the Vindhya range from Bhopâl, one may see on the side of the road, upon a spur of the hill, a singular pillar of sandstone rising in two spires, one turning and rising above the other to the height of some twenty to thirty feet. On the spur of a hill, half a mile distant, is another sandstone pillar not quite so high. The tradition is that the smaller pillar was the affianced bride of the larger one, who was a youth of a family of great eminence in those parts. Coming with his uncle to pay his first visit to his bride in the marriage procession, he grew more and more impatient as he approached nearer and nearer, and she shared

> the feeling. At last, unable to restrain himself, he jumped from his uncle's shoulders, and looked with all his might towards the place where his bride was said to be seated. Unhappily she felt no less impatient than he did, and they saw each other at the same moment. In that moment the bride, bridegroom, and uncle were, all three, converted into pillars, and there they stand to this day, a monument to warn mankind against an inclination to indulge in curiosity. It is a singular fact that in one of the most extensive tribes of the Gond population, to which this couple is said to have belonged, the bride always, contrary to the usual Hindu custom, goes to the bridegroom in procession to prevent a calamity.

(W. H. Sleeman, *Rambles and Recollections of an Indian Official*, Oxford, 1915, vol. 1, p. 123, and cf. Edwin Sidney Hartland, *The Legend of Perseus: A Study of Traditions in Story, Custom and Belief*, vol. 3, London, 1896, p. 133.)

And compare Crooke's *Religion and Folklore of Northern India*, New Delhi, 1925, pp. 170–171:

> The curses of deified men are highly dangerous. A famous saint appeared at the great city of Valabhi, now ruined, in Kāthiawār, but no one, save a potter's wife, would cook for him. So he cursed the city and warned the potter and his wife to leave the city, and he adjured the woman not to look back. But when she reached the seashore she, like Lot's wife, disobeyed the order, and she was turned into a pillar of stone. At that moment Valabhi was destroyed, (A. K. Forbes, *Rasmala or Hindu Annals of the Province of Goozerat*, London, 1878, p. 14). The taboo against looking back appears in many tales: when the goddess Chandesvari was invited to come to Southern India she warned the Brahmans to walk in front and not to look back, but they disobeyed the order and she refused to move further; in a Kashmīr tale the hero is warned not to look back lest he should be changed into a pillar of stone; mourners in Northern India on

> leaving the cremation ground dare not look back lest their souls may be detained by the dead, (E. Thurston, *Castes and Tribes on Southern India*, Madras, 1909, p. 171; J. H. Knowles, *Folk-Tales of Kashmir*, London, 1889, p. 401; *North Indian Notes and Queries*, vol. 2, Allahabad, 1892, p. 10, vol. 5, 1895, p. 185). See also E. S. Hartland, *The Legend of Perseus*, vol. 3, London, 1896, p. 132, the story of the Hindu saint Sri Dharamnathji, whose servant's wife on looking back was turned into stone (W. Crooke, ed., *North Indian Notes and Queries*, Allahabad, 119, quoting Forbes, *Rás Mala*; and ibid., pp. 133, 134–147 for further examples of petrification.

Furthermore, it is interesting to compare this motif with what is found in Edgar Thurston's *Castes and Tribes of Southern India*, vol. 7, Madras, 1909, p. 171, where he brings a Togata legend which reads as follows:

> Once upon a time, a king from Southern India went on a pilgrimage with his wife to Banares. While there, he unwittingly incurred a nameless but heinous pollution. Horrified, he applied to some Brāhmans there to purify him, promising them half his kingdom in return. They asked for some tangible record of his promise, and the king called upon the goddess Chaudēsvari, who had a temple nearby, to witness his oath. The purification was effected, and he departed home. Later on the Brāhmans came south, and asked for the fulfillment of his promise. The king declared that he could not remember having made any such undertaking. The Brāhmans accordingly went to Benares, and asked Chaudēsvari to come south, and bear witness to the king's oaths. She agreed, on the usual condition that they should go in front, and not look back at her as she came. As happens in other stories of the same kind, they are said to have broken the condition. At Nandavaram they looked back, and the goddess instantly stopped, and remained immoveable. A temple was built for her there, and the Brāhmans remained in the south, and

still take part in the worship of Chaudēsvari which the Togatas inaugurate, even though she is not one of the Hindu pantheon, and delights in animal sacrifice.....

See also R. E. Enthoven, *Folklore of Gujarat*, Bombay, 1964, p. 58:

The following tradition is connected with a place, about a mile from Dhhank, called Dhhank-ni Fui. Dhhank was in ancient times a great city and was known as *Preh Pātant.* Once a *bāvā* (recluse), named Dhundhalimal, came to reside with his *chelā* (disciple) in a cave on a neighbouring hill. Every day the *chelā* went about the city begging alms for himself and his *guru*; but nobody except a poor *kumbhāran* (a potter-woman) ever gave him anything. So the *chelā* was obliged to cut and sell fuel in order to obtain means of subsistence, although he did not mention this fact to his *guru.* One day the *guru* noticed the growing baldness of his disciple and on being questioned about it, the latter had to admit his difficulties in earning a livelihood. The next day the *bāvā* decided to test the charity of the neighbourhood, and went on a begging round in person. He moved about the city from door to door, crying aloud *ālek ālek*, but nobody except the *kumbhār* woman offered him so much as a handful of flour. He then addressed the latter thus:–"Girl, this city is sinful and will shortly meet with destruction. Fly, therefore, instantly with your family and never turn your face towards the city in your flight". Having thus warned the only righteous person in the city, the *bāvā* returned to his cave where, after reciting an incantation in high exasperation, he pronounced a terrible curse for the destruction of the city 'Let Pātan be buried and let *māyā* (i.e., the unreal splendour of the city) be reduced to *māti* (dust).' A whirlwind at once arose and destroyed the whole city. The *kumbhāran* had already fled with her children; but she unfortunately happened to look back in her flight, in spite of the warning, and she and her children were all turned into stones. In this form she can be seen even to-day, with two of her children on her shoulders and leading the other two.

Cf. ibid., p. 64.

See further on the petrification of people in Verrier Elwin, *Folk-Tales of Mahakoshal*, Oxford University Press, 1944, pp. 213–214.

Finally, I may add what I found in Edwin Sidney Hartland, *The Legend of Perseus*, vol. 3, London, 1896, p. 132:

> There are cases, however, in which the crime of looking back in disobedience to an express taboo has been punished by petrifaction, and where the connection with Lot's wife is by no means so easily proved. Once upon a time the Hindu saint, Sri Dharamnathji, was doing penance in the jungle near Pattan. His disciple Gharibnáthji used to beg alms in the city, but as the people were not charitable he was obliged to maintain himself by carrying bundles of firewood and selling them in the town. From the proceeds he purchased flour, which a shepherd's wife baked for him, adding a loaf from herself. The sage, "observing the bald patch on his disciple's head caused by the loads he carried, cursed the city to be swallowed up. He had previously warned the shepherd's wife to leave the place and not look back. The city was swallowed up; and the woman, disobeying the saint's command, was turned into a stone."
>
> *N. Ind. N. and Q.*, 119, quoting Forbes, *Rás Mála*.

On the petrification of evil people, see *The Travels of Ibn Battutah* (1325–1354), ed. T. Mackintosh-Smith, London, 2002, p. 154:

> I rode out one day with Ála al-Mulk, and we came to a plain called Tarna, seven miles from Lahari, where I saw an innumerable quantity of stones resembling the shapes of men and animals. Many of them were disfigured and their forms effaced, but there remained among them also the shapes of grains of wheat, chickpeas, beans and lentils, and there were

remains of a city wall and house walls. We saw too the ruins of a house with a chamber of hewn stones, in the midst of which there was a platform of hewn stones resembling a single block, surmounted by a human figure, except that its head was elongated and its mouth on the side of its face and its hands behind its back like a pinioned captive. The place had pools of stinking water and an inscription on one of its walls in Indian characters. 'Ala al-Mulk told me that the historians assert that in this place there was a great city whose inhabitants were so given to depravity that they were turned to stone, and that it is their king who is on the platform in the house we have described, which is still called "the king's palace." They add that the inscription on one of the stones there in Indian characters gives the date of the destruction of the people of that city, which occurred about a thousand years ago .

Cf. *The Travels of Ibn Battuta in the Near East, Asia and Africa, 1325–1354*, trans. and ed. Samuel Lee, London, 1829, p. 102, for a more literal version of this passage.

10. Two *Akedah* Stories

I think we are all acquainted with the rather troubling story of the *Akedah*, related in *Genesis* chapter 22, where Abraham is ordered to sacrifice his one and only son Isaac, and he agrees to do so. There is a somewhat gruesome parallel in the *Mahābārata* 13:3, as related in J. M. Macfie's abridgment in his *Myths and Legends of India: An Introduction to the Study of Hinduism*, New Delhi, 1993, chapter XXXII. There we read how the king of Benares named Shivi, who was always willing to hear the cry of a supplicant, was once called upon by a Brāhmin.

> When Shivi appeared and, after the usual salutations, asked the holy man what he would like to eat, the Brāhmin answered, "I should like to eat your son. Kill him yourself and prepare his flesh with your own hands. When everything is ready, come and tell me." Without a moment's hesitation, Shivi killed and cooked his son. And when the meal was ready, he went in search of the Brāhmin to summon him to his horrid repast. At the palace gate he met some of his servants, who told him that the Brāhmin had set the palace on fire and that the female apartments and the stables, in which his horses and elephants were kept, had been burned to the ground. Shivi listened to this heart-rending report with the utmost calmness. He showed not the least signs of anger. He didn't even change colour. At that very moment the Brāhmin appeared. No word of reproach,

> no sign of impatience, indicated that the monarch was in the least annoyed. He merely said, "Sir, your food is ready. Will you do me the honour of coming to the guest-chamber?" The Brāhmin accordingly accompanied his host to the room where the food had been set forth. But he did not sit down, or make any attempt to begin. Instead, he turned to the king and said, "I do not want any of this food. It is you who must eat the meal you have prepared." And even this command the monarch was prepared to obey, because it was the command of a Brāhmin.

But the story has a happy ending, as does *Akedat Yitzhak*:

> He therefore sat down before the dish containing his own son's flesh and was about to eat it, when the Brāhmin seized his hand. "Of a truth," he explained, "there is nobody like you. I have tried you and tested you. I ordered you to kill your son and to cook his flesh. I have burned down your palace, your zenana and your stables. You have obeyed my every injunction. You have not shown the least anger or resentment. What a difficult thing I asked you to do it. You are manifestly willing to give anything to Brāhmin."[29]
>
> As he listened to the Brāhmin's words of commendation, Shivi happened to look up and saw his son, whom he had killed and cooked, standing before him. The prince had never looked so beautiful. There was about him an ampler, a more divine appearance than belongs to mortals. When the father took his son in his arms, the Brāhmin disappeared. But those who tell the tale say he was not an ordinary Brāhmin, but the creator himself, who came in mortal guise to put the monarch to a searching proof, more testing even than that by which Indra and Agni had tried him and failed.

---

29. See David Shulman, *The Hungry God: Hindu Tales of Filicide and Devotion, Chicago and London, 1993, for a penetrating examination of the "Akedah" theme in certain South Indian legends.*

(Macfie, ibid., pp. 242–243, and this was actually his second trial, see ibid., pp. 238–242.)

> "How was it, O king," they cried, "that you were able to achieve such an impossible task? How did you persuade yourself to kill and cook the heir to your throne?" To this question Shivi replied: "I did it, not for the sake of happiness. I did it, because it was the right thing to do, and it has always been my earnest resolve to do what is right."

The similarities are potently apparent, as are the moral perplexities.[30] They have troubled generations of commentators, as evidenced in the wonderful study of Shalom Spiegel, *The Last Trial: On the Legends and Lore of the Command to Abraham to Offer Isaac as a Sacrifice: The Akedah*, New York, 1969.[31] We shall not address ourselves to these weighty questions, only merely point to the apparent parallelism between these two distant legends. But let us briefly note that according to some rabbinic traditions Abraham did actually sacrifice Isaac, his son, and perhaps even burned him on the altar,[32] but afterwards he was miraculously brought back to life.

This is yet another Indian myth that has partial parallelism to the

30. See, e.g., Lippman Bodoff, *The Binding of Isaac, Religion, Murders, and Kabbalah: Seeds of Jewish Extremism and Alienation?* Jerusalem and New York, 2005, pp. 67 et seq.

31. See also Aharon Agus, *The Binding of Isaac and Messiah: Law, Martyrdom and Deliverance in Early Rabbinic Religiosity*, New York, 1988; *The Sacrifice of Isaac in the Three Monotheistic Religions*, ed. Fredric Manns, Jerusalem, 1995; Jon D. Levenson, *The Death and Resurrection of the Beloved Son: The Transformation of Child Sacrifice in Judaism and Christianity*, New Haven and London, 1993; Y. A. Efrati, *Parashat ha-Akedah: Ha-Mikraot u-Midrashei ha-Aggadah shel Hazal ki-Fshutam*, Petah Tikvah, 1983, etc.

32. See Spiegel, ibid., pp. 46 et seq., and note especially Ibn Ezra's comment to *Genesis* 22:19 that if, indeed, Abraham slaughtered his son, "he acted contrary to Scripture" (Spiegel, ibid., p. 47). On "the ashes of Isaac," in addition to the "blood of the *Akedah*," see ibid., p. 57. Furthermore, the parallelism is further sharpened by the comparisons with the pascal lamb which was both sacrificed and eaten. See Spiegel, ibid., pp. 52 et seq.

Akedah story, but also significant differences. It is the sacred history of Śunaḥsépa as found in *Aitareya Brāhmaṇa* 7:13–18 (33:1–6), with various parallels, cited in full in R. Panikkar's *Myth, Faith and Hermeneutics: Cross-Cultural Studies*, New York, 1947, pp. 106–125 (with bibliographic references pp. 173–174, notes 8–15).

In brief: Hariścandra had many wives but no son. So he begs Veruna to grant him a son, and Varuna agrees and Rohita is born. But then Varuna demands of Hariścandra to sacrifice his son to him. Hariścandra prevaricates and delays the sacrifice, until he can no longer do so. Rohita then leaves home and wanders for many years until he too can no longer delay the sacrifice, so he finds a substitute in one Sunaḥsepa, the youngest son of a seer Ajigarta Sauyavasi, who is willing to sell his son for one hundred cows. In this way Rohita finds a substitute to sacrifice, with the agreement of Varuna. Śunaḥsépa is brought to the altar, but no one is willing to bind, except his father Ajigarta for another hundred cows. He is bound and prays to many different gods, each one passing him on to another, until finally with Indra's advice he prays and praises the Asrins and Usas (Twin Gods, and Goddess of Dawn) who loosen his bonds and free him, and this with Varuna's agreement. Finally, an alternative type of sacrifice with *Soma* is offered to the gods.....

In their myth too a son is requested for god, and granted, only to be ordered to be sacrificed. But here the father is unwilling, and offers a substitute human offering, which is accepted. But the human substitute offering finds a way to redeem himself, and a different, more morally acceptable offering is made.

The similarities are potent, but the moral differences even more so. And see Panilzka's interpretation of his myth, ibid., pp. 125–127, for what he calls the "*locus classicus of discussion on human sacrifice in Vedic India*" (p. 134), which clearly is only one of the possible ways of understanding this story (see ibid., p. 179, note 98).

11. A Third *Akedah* Story

THIS ONE COMES from Alice Elizabeth Dracott's *Simla Village Tales*, London, 1906, pp. 194–198, and is entitled "Tabaristan." The points of similarity are so obvious that they need no comment. Simla (Shimla) is, of course, a town in Himachal Pradesh.

> In a country called Tabaristan there lived a rich Raja, who gave a feast and invited a number of guests. Amongst the guests came a stranger who partook of the good things distributed. The Raja seeing him, enquired who he was. "I am a stranger," said he, "but am willing to serve you, as I have come from a distant country." The Raja said he would keep him as a *Chowdikar*, to guard his house at night, so all night long the stranger used to pace up and down the Palace grounds keeping watch.
>
> One night the Raja came out, and seeing him pacing up and down, asked him who he was. "Why, I am he who you engaged as a servant." Hardly had he spoken when a loud cry echoed through the ground, and a voice said, "I am going on, I am going on." "What is that?" asked the Raja. "I do not know", said the man, "but I have it every night." "Go and find out," returned the Raja. So the man turned to do his bidding.
>
> Now the Raja was very curious, and quickly wrapping himself in his coat, quietly followed his servant. Outside the garden gate sat a figure covered and clothed in loose white garments. On

approaching it the servant said, "Who are you?" "I am time," replied the figure, "and hold the Raja's life, which is nearly over." "Cannot anything be done to spare it?" asked the man. "Yes, it can be spared by the sacrifice of another, and that one must be your son." "I will not only give my son's life, but the lives of all my family and my own," replied the man; "but if you want only my son, you may have him." Then he went and told his son, who said: "Gladly will I give my life, for what is it in comparison with the life of a Raja? Come father, take me soon that I may die."

Then the man led his son to the veiled figure and said: "Here is my son; he is willing to die." Taking the knife, he was about to plunge it into his son when the figure cried out, "Enough! You have proved that you were willing not only to give your son, but your whole family, and the Almighty is pleased to spare the Raja's life for another seven years."

Now the Raja who had heard every word of the interview, quickly returned to the spot where he had first heard the voice, and there awaited his servant's return. "Well, what was the sound?" asked he, when he saw him. "A man and a woman had quarreled," replied the servant, "but I had managed to reconcile them, and they have promised not to quarrel for seven years." Then the Raja left him, and ordered him to appear at the court the following day.

Next day, when the court was full, the Raja addressed all his people and said, "I am resolved to give up my throne and all I possess to this man for last night, unknown to me, he was willing to give up, not only his son's life, but his own, and the lives of all his family, in order to save mine, and for my sake." The poor servant was deeply touched and astonished at the turn matters had so unexpectedly taken, but the Raja was firm in his resolve, and left his throne and his kingdom. The servant became Raja, and ruled wisely to the end of his days.

12. "It is not done in our place to give the younger before the first-born" (*Genesis* 30:26)

In Genesis chapter 29 we read how Jacob served Laban as a bondsman for many years in order to obtain in marriage Rachel. But first he was given Leah as she was the oldest and Laban claimed that he was not allowed to marry off the younger before the elder. Since he was penniless, he had to work many (twenty) years to pay Laban for his daughters.

Among the Assamese, according to John Butler, *A Sketch of Assam with some Account of the Hill Tribes*, London, 1847, pp. 142 et seq., in Assam a man may marry two sisters, but he must marry the elder before the younger. It is not uncommon when a man is poverty-stricken to engage, live, and work for several years for the father of the girl he wishes to marry. He is then called a *Chapunea*, a kind of bondsman, and is entitled to receive *bhat kupper*, food, and clothing, but no wages. It is at the expiration of the period of servitude, if the girl does not dislike him, the marriage takes place. The man is looked upon in the family as a *lchanu damad* (or son-in-law) and is treated kindly.

13. *Genesis* 34 and the Vettuvan Caste

In *Genesis* 34, we read the story of Dinah, the daughter of Jacob, who caught the attention of Shechem, the son of Hamor, who became infatuated by her, and asked her hand in marriage. The sons of Jacob agreed on condition the whole tribe be circumcised, to which Hamor agreed. On the third day after they were all circumcised and sick with pain, two sons of Jacob, Shimon and Levi, came and slaughtered them all.

Compare the legend found in Thurston, vol. 7, p. 396 (the Vettuvan caste), as follows:

> It is related that one of their tribe went and asked a high-caste Nāyar to give him a daughter in marriage. The Nāyar offered to do so on condition that the whole tribe would come to his place and dance on berries, each one who fell to be shot with arrows. The tribe foolishly agreed to the condition, and went and danced, with the result that, as each one tripped and fell, he or she was mercilessly shot dead with arrows. A little girl who survived this treatment was secretly rescued, and taken away by a compassionate Nāyar, who married her into his family. From this union, the present day Vēttuvans affirm their origin is to be traced.

14. Joseph and the Wife of Potiphar

GENESIS 39 DESCRIBES this well-known story of the unfortunate adventure of Joseph who refused the advances of Potiphar's wife and was subsequently imprisoned when she accused him of raping her. Compare the Vīramushti caste's legend, related in E. Thurston's *Castes and Tribes of Southern India*, Madras, 1909, vol. 7, p. 408:

> .... From that time Chikayya became a new man and a true Jangam, and went from place to place visiting sacred shrines. One day he happened to be at a place where lived a merchant prince, who never dined except in the company of a Jangam. On the suggestion of his wife Nīlakuntaladēvi, an invitation to dine was sent to Chikayya, who accepted it. After dinner, the merchant went out on business, and Nīlakuntaladēvi, noticing what a beautiful man Chikayya was, fell in love with him. He, however, rejected her advances, and ran away, leaving his knapsack behind him. Nīlakuntaladēvi cut off her golden necklace, and, having placed it in the knapsack, ran after Chikayya, and threw it at him, asking him to accept it. She then inflicted several cuts on herself, and, as soon as her husband returned home, complained that the Jangam had stolen her necklace, and attempted to ravish her. Information was sent to Basayya, the head of the mutt, and a council meeting summoned, at which it was decided that Chikayya should have

> his head cut off. The order to carry out this act was given to the Vīramushtis, who went in search of him, and at last found him beneath the shade of a tree overhanging the bank of a river, engaged in worshipping his linga, which was in his hand. On searching the knapsack, they found the necklace, and proceeded to cut off Chikayya's head, which went several hundred feet up into the air, and travelled towards the mutt, whither the headless trunk followed on foot.

The continuation ends on a happier note when Siva reunites his head and body, etc. (p. 409). Cf. above note 5.

15. Moses in the Bulrushes

THE STORY OF how Moses was placed in "an ark of bulrushes," which was daubed "with slime and pitch" and placed in a river, etc. (*Exodus* 2:1–11) is well known to all. Theodor H. Gaster, in his *Myth, Legend, and Custom in the Old Testament: A Comparative Study with Chapters from Sir James Frazer's "Folklore in the Old Testament,"* vol. 1, 1975, pp. 224–230, 380–383, has identified many parallel or similar legends and myths from around the world, but also from Indian sources. He remarks (p. 226) that:

> It is by no means impossible that the Biblical writer was acquainted with this earlier story, and modeled his own narrative upon it. On the other hand, both the Mesopotamian and the Hebrew tales may equally well be regarded as independent offshoots from the common root of popular imagination; and this view is supported by the occurrence of a parallel legend in the great Indian epic, the *Mahabharata,* since it is hardly likely that the authors of that work knew anything of Semitic traditions.

He then continues to tell us the Indian traditions beginning with the *Mahabharata* story as follows (transl. R. C. Roy, second ed., pp. 651 et seq.):

> The poet relates how the king's daughter Kunti or Pritha was

> beloved by the Sun-god and bore him a son "beautiful as a celestial," "clad in armour, adorned with brilliant golden earrings, endued with leonine eyes and bovine shoulders." But ashamed of her frailty, and dreading the anger of her royal father and mother, the princess, "in consultation with her nurse, placed her child in a waterproof basket, covered all over with sheets, made of wicker-work, smooth, comfortable and furnished with a beautiful pillow. And with tearful eyes she consigned it to (the waters of) the river Asva." Having done so, she returned to the palace, heavy at heart, lest her angry sire should learn her secret. But the basket containing the babe floated down the river till it came to the Ganges and was washed ashore at the city of Champa in the Suta territory. There it chanced that a man of the Suta tribe and his wife, walking on the bank of the river, saw the basket, drew it from the water, and on opening it beheld a baby boy "(beautiful) as the morning sun, clad in a golden armour, and with a beautiful face adorned with brilliant earrings." Now the pair were childless, and when the roan looked upon the fair infant, he said to his wife, "Surely, considering that I have no son, the gods have sent this child to me." So they adopted him, and brought him up, and he became a mighty archer, and his name was Kama. But his royal mother had news of him through her spies.

He then brings us yet another parallel from Ghulam Muhammad, found in *Memoirs of the Asiatic Society of Bengal* 1/7, 1905, pp. 124 et seq., as follows:

> A similar story is told of the exposure and upbringing of Trakhan, the famous sixteenth-century king of Gilgit, a town situated at a height of about five thousand feet above the sea in the very heart of the snowy Himalayas. His father Tra-Trakhan had married a woman of a wealthy family at Darel. Being passionately devoted to polo, the king was in the habit of going over to Darel every week to play his favourite game with the seven brothers of his

wife. One day, so keen were they all on the sport, they agreed to play on condition that the winner should put the losers to death. The contest was long and skilful, but at last the king won the match, and agreeably to the compact he, like a true sportsman, put his seven brothers-in-law to death. When he came home, no doubt in high spirits, and told the queen the result of the match, with its painful but necessary sequel, she was so far from sharing in his glee that she actually resented the murder, or rather the execution, of her seven brothers and resolved to avenge it. So she put arsenic in the king's food, which soon laid him out, and the queen reigned in his stead. Now it so happened that at the time she was with child by the king, and about a month afterwards gave birth to a son and called his name Trakhan. But so deeply did she mourn the death of her brothers, that she could not bear to look on the child of their murderer; hence she locked the infant in a wooden box and secretly threw it into the river. The current swept the box down the river as far as Hodar, a village in the Chilas District. Now it chanced that, as it floated by, two poor brothers were gathering sticks on the bank; and, thinking that the chest might contain treasure, one of them plunged into the water and drew it ashore. In order not to excite the covetousness of others by a display of the expected treasure, they hid the chest in a bundle of faggots and carried it home. There they opened it, and what was their surprise to discover in it a lovely babe still alive. Their mother brought up the little foundling with every care; and it seemed as if the infant brought a blessing to the house, for whereas they had been poor before, they now grew richer and richer, and set down their prosperity to the windfall of the child in the chest. When the boy was twelve years old, he conceived a great longing to go to Gilgit, of which he had beard much. So he went with his two fosterbrothers, but on the way they stayed for a few days at a place called Baldas on the top of a hill. Now his mother was still queen of Gilgit, but she had fallen very ill, and as there was none to succeed her in Gilgit the people were searching for a king to come from elsewhere and reign over them. One morning, while things were in this state and all minds were in suspense, it chanced that the village cocks crew, but instead of saying as usual "Cock-a-doodle-do" they said "*Beldas tham bayi,*" which being interpreted means, "There is a king at Baldas." So men were at once sent to bring down any stranger they might find there. The messengers found the three brothers and brought them before the queen. As Trakhan was handsome and stately, the queen addressed herself to him, and in course of conversation elicited from him his story. To her surprise and joy she learned that this goodly boy was her own lost son, whom on a rash impulse of grief and resentment she had cast into the river. So she embraced him and proclaimed him the rightful heir to the kingdom of Gilgit.

Otto Rank, in his *The Myth of the Birth of the Hero*, ed. Philip Freund, New York, 1932, adds the following observation, pp. 19–20:

A striking resemblance to the entire structure of the Karna legend is presented by the birth history of Ion, the ancestor of the Ionians. The following account is based on a relatively late tradition.

Apollo, in the grotto of the rock of the Athenian Acropolis, procreated a son with Creusa, the daughter of Erechtheus. In this grotto the boy was also born, and exposed; the mother leaves the child behind in a woven basket, in the hope that Apollo will not leave his son to perish. At Apollo's request, Hermes carries the child the same night to Delphi, where the priestess finds him on the threshold of the temple in the morning. She brings the boy up, and when he has grown into a youth makes hi m a servant of the temple. Erechtheus later gave his daughter Creusa in marriage to Xuthus. As the marriage long remained childless, they addressed the Delphian oracle, praying to be blessed with progeny. The god reveals to Xuthus that the first to meet him on leaving the sanctuary is his son. He hastens outside and meets

> the youth, whom he joyfully greets as his own son, giving him the name Ion, which means "walker." Creusa refuses to accept the youth as her son; her attempt to poison him fails, and the infuriated people turn against her. Ion is about to attack her, but Apollo, who does not wish the son to kill his own mother, enlightens the mind of the priestess so that she understands the connection. By means of the basket in which the newborn child had lain, Creusa recognizes him as her son, and reveals to him the secret of his birth.

Here I should like to add yet another (partial) parallel, again from the Indian sub-continent, which, I believe, has gone hitherto unnoticed. It comes from Hemacandra's *The Lives of the Jain Elders*, transl. R. C. Fynes, Oxford, New York, 1998, Canto 2, pp. 55–56. Hemacandra lived from 1089 till 1172 in the Gujarat, and was a Jain monk (p. X.), and wrote many books, his last major one being *The Lives of the Jain Elders* (p. XI), which is both legendary as well as moralistic. *The Story of Kuberadatta* contains the following episode, which tells how the prostitute Kuberasena conceived twins, a boy and a girl, which her mother told her she must get rid of.

> 231 Her mother said to the prostitute, "These twins are your enemies; while they were in your womb, they brought you to death's door.
> 232 Breast-feeding these twins will take away your youth, and the youth of prostitutes is their livelihood; protect your youth, as your life!
> 233 Child, this pair of twins is like a turd fallen from your womb. Throw it out! This is our custom, after all."
> 234 The prostitute said, "Although that is the case, please be patient, mother. I shall nourish the twins for ten days."
> 235 In the end, the prostitute was given permission by her mother, and she nourished the babies, suckling them day and night.

236 And as she thus looked after the children day and night, the eleventh day dawned, looking like a night of death.
237 She had two rings made and engraved with the names Kuberadatta and Kuberadattā, and put them on their fingers.
238 With breaking heart, she made a wooden chest, filled it with jewels, and placed the two babies in it.
239 She herself let the chest float away in the current of the river Yamunā, and it travelled free from harm, floating like a duck.
240 Then Kuberasenā turned and went home, having given a libation to her children with the tears from her eyes.
241 The chest arrived at the gate of the city Śaurya which faced onto the River Yamunā. Two sons of wealthy merchants saw and grabbed it.
242 And when they saw the baby boy and the baby girl inside it, one took the boy, and the other took the girl.
243 And by inspecting the writing on the rings on the babies' fingers, they discovered that they were called Kuberadatta and Kuberadattā.
244 They both grew up in the houses of the two rich men, and were protected by them as carefully as a deposit entrusted by a powerful man.

The continuation is tragic and moralistic but not relevant to this study.

Yet another sort of parallel may be found in N. M. Penzer's *The Ocean of Story*, vol. 2, London, 1924, pp. 4–5:

Story of the Hypercritical Ascetic

On the bank of the Ganges there is a city named Mākandikā; in that city long ago there was a certain ascetic who observed a vow of silence, and he lived on alms, and, surrounded by numerous other holy beggars, dwelt in a monastery within the precincts of a god's temple where he had taken up his abode. Once, when he entered a certain merchant's house to beg, he saw a beautiful maiden coming out with alms in her hand, and the rascal, seeing that she was wonderfully beautiful, was smitten with love, and exclaimed: "Ah! Ah! Alas!" And that merchant overheard him. Then, taking the alms he had received, he departed to his own house; and then the merchant went there and said to him in his astonishment: "Why did you to-day suddenly break your vow of silence and say what you did?" When he heard that the ascetic said to the merchant: "This daughter of yours has inauspicious marks; when she marries, you will undoubtedly perish, wife, sons and all. So, when I saw her, I was afflicted, for you are my devoted adherent; and thus it was on your account that I broke silence and said what I did. So place this daughter of yours by night in a basket, on the top of which there must be a light, and set her adrift on the Ganges." The merchant said, "So I will," and went away; and at night he did all he had been directed to do, out of pure fear. The timid are ever unreflecting.

The hermit for his part said at that time to his own pupils: "Go to the Ganges, and when you see a basket floating along with a light on the top of it, bring it here secretly, but you must not open it, even if you hear a noise inside." They said, "We will do so," and off they went; but before they reached the Ganges, strange to say, a certain prince went into the river to bathe. He, seeing that basket, which the merchant had thrown in, by the help of the light on it, got his servants to fetch it for him, and immediately opened it out of curiosity. And in it he saw that heartenchanting girl, and he married her on the spot by the *gāndharva* ceremony of marriage. And he set the basket adrift on the Ganges, exactly as it was before, putting a lamp on the top of it, and placing a fierce monkey inside it.

The prince having departed with that pearl of maidens, the pupils of the hermit came there in the course of their search, and saw that basket, and took it up and carried it to the hermit. Then he, being delighted, said to them: "I will take this upstairs and perform incantations with it alone, but you must lie in silence this night." When he had said this, the ascetic took the basket to the top of the monastery and opened it, eager to behold the merchant's daughter. And then a monkey of terrible appearance sprang out of it, and rushed upon the ascetic, like his own immoral conduct incarnate in bodily form. The monkey in its fury immediately tore off with its teeth the nose of the wicked ascetic, and his ears with its claws, as if it had been a skilful executioner; and in that state the ascetic ran downstairs, and when his pupils beheld him they could with difficulty suppress their laughter. And early next morning everybody heard the story, and laughed heartily; but the merchant was delighted, and his daughter also, as she had obtained a good husband.

Penzer adds the following (ibid., note 1):

> Cf. [Rachel Harriette Busk, ed.] *Sagas from the Far East*: [*or, Kalmouk and Mongolian Traditionary Tales*], tale xi, pp. 123, 124. Here the crime contemplated is murder, and the ape is represented by a tiger. The story bears a certain resemblance to the termination of "Alles aus einer Erbse," Kaden's *Unter den Olivenbäumen*, Leipzig, 1880, p. 22. See also pp. 75 and 220 of the same collection. In the *Pentamerone* of Basile ([R. F.] Burton, [*le Pentamerone: or The Tale of Tales*…], vol. I, [London 1893] second diversion of the third day, p. 149 et seq.) a princess is set afloat in a box and found by a king, whose wife she eventually becomes. See also [C. H.] Tawney's *The Kathākoça*, [*or, Treasury of Stories*] London 1895, pp. 131–134.

16. Young Moses' Test

For the sake of convenience I shall cite a well-known Midrash relating to Moses' early youth in Pharaoh's palace from Louis Ginzberg's magisterial *The Legends of the Jews*, vol. 2, Philadelphia, 1910, pp. 272–274 (omitting certain sections):

Moses Rescued by Gabriel

> When Moses was in his third year, Pharaoh was dining one day, with the queen Alfar'anit at his right hand, his daughter Bithiah with the infant Moses upon her lap at his left, and Balaam the son of Beor together with his two sons and all the princes of the realm sitting at table in the king's presence. It happened that the infant took the crown from off the king's head, and placed it on his own. When the king and the princes saw this, they were terrified, and each one in turn expressed his astonishment. The king said unto the princes, "What speak you, and what say you, O ye princes, on this matter, and what is to be done to this Hebrew boy on account of this act?"
>
> Balaam spoke, saying: "Remember now, O my lord and king, the dream which thou didst dream many days ago, and how thy servant interpreted it unto thee. Now this is a child of the Hebrews in whom is the spirit of God. Let not my lord the king imagine in his heart that being a child he did the thing without knowledge. For he is a Hebrew boy, and wisdom and

understanding are with him, although he is yet a child, and with wisdom has he done this, and chosen unto himself the kingdom of Egypt. For this is the manner of all the Hebrews, to deceive kings and their magnates, to do all things cunningly in order to make the kings of the earth and their men to stumble.

"Surely thou knowest that Abraham their father acted thus, who made the armies of Nimrod king of Babel and of Abimelech king of Gerar to stumble, and he possessed himself of the land of the children of Heth and the whole realm of Canaan. Their father Abraham went down into Egypt, and said of Sarah his wife, She is my sister, in order to make Egypt and its king to stumble.

"His son Isaac did likewise when he went to Gerar, and he dwelt there, and his strength prevailed over the army of Abimelech, and he intended to make the kingdom of the Philistines to stumble, by saying that Rebekah his wife was his sister.

"Jacob also dealt treacherously with his brother, and took his birthright and his blessing from him. Then he went to Paddan-Aram, to Laban, his mother's brother, and he obtained his daughters from him cunningly, and also his cattle and all his belongings, and he fled away and returned to the land of Canaan, to his father.

"His sons sold their brother Joseph, and he went down into Egypt and became a slave, and he was put into prison for twelve years, until the former Pharaoh delivered him from the prison, and magnified him above all the princes of Egypt on account of his interpreting the king's dreams: When God caused a famine to descend upon the whole world, Joseph sent for his father, and he brought him down into Egypt his father, his brethren, and all his father's household, and he supplied them with food without pay or reward, while he acquired Egypt, and made slaves of all its inhabitants.

"Now, therefore, my lord king, behold, this child has risen up in their stead in Egypt, to do according to their deeds and make sport of every man, be he king, prince, or judge. If it please the

> king, let us now spill his blood upon the ground, lest he grow up and snatch the government from thine hand, and the hope of Egypt be cut off after he reigns. Let us, moreover, call for all the judges and the wise men of Egypt, that we may know whether the judgment of death be due to this child, as I have said, and then we will slay him."
>
> Pharaoh sent and called for all the wise men of Egypt, and they came, and the angel Gabriel was disguised as one of them. When they were asked their opinion in the matter, Gabriel spoke up, and said: "If it please the king, let him place an onyx stone before the child, and a coal of fire, and if he stretches out his hand and grasps the onyx stone, then shall we know that the child hath done with wisdom all that he hath done, and we will slay him. But if he stretches out his hand and grasps the coal of fire, then shall we know that it was not with consciousness that he did the thing, and he shall live."
>
> The counsel seemed good in the eyes of the king, and when they had placed the stone and the coal before the child, Moses stretched forth his hand toward the onyx stone and attempted to seize it, but the angel Gabriel guided his hand away from it and placed it upon the live coal, and the coal burnt the child's hand, and he lifted it up and touched it to his mouth, and burnt part of his lips and part of his tongue, and for all his life he became slow of speech and of a slow tongue.
>
> Seeing this, the king and the princes knew that Moses had not acted with knowledge in taking the crown from off the king's head, and they refrained from slaying him.[33]

Interestingly enough, when perusing Edgar Thurston's *Castes and Tribes of Southern India*, vol. 7, Madras, 1909, on the section on the Tiyan, p. 73, I came across the following passage:

---

33. Cf. Ginzberg's comments in vol. 5, Philadelphia, 1925, p. 402, note 65, for the various sources and versions of this legend.

When a child is provided by nature with teeth, it is the subject of a little ceremony, during which it is expected to disclose its natural propensities. The usual mat and other articles are arranged, and there are in addition a large flat bell-metal plate containing a rice cake, a knife, a palmyra leaf grantham (book), a cocoanut, and a gold ornament. The child is let loose, and allowed to pick out anything from the plate. If it takes the cake, it will be greedy; if the knife, brave; if the book, learned; if the cocoanut, a landlord; and if the gold ornament, rich.

17. Moses, the Storks, and the Serpents

In Louis Ginzberg's *The Legends of the Jews,* vol. 2, Philadelphia, 1910, pp. 286–287, we read as follows:

> Moses was twenty-seven years old when he became king over Ethiopia, and he reigned for forty years. On the seventh day of his reign, all the people assembled and came before him, to ask his counsel as to what was to be done to the city they were besieging. The king answered them, and said: "If you will hearken to my words, the city will be delivered into our hands. Proclaim with a loud voice throughout the whole camp, unto all the people, saying: 'Thus saith the king! Go to the forest and fetch hither of the young of the stork, each man one fledgling in his hand. And if there be any man that transgresseth the word of the king, not to bring a bird, he shall die, and the king shall take all belonging to him.' And when you have brought them, they shall be in your keeping. You shall rear them until they grow up, and you shall teach them to fly as the hawk flieth."
>
> All the people did according to the word of Moses, and after the young storks had grown to full size, he ordered them to be starved for three days. On the third day the king said unto them, "Let every man put on his armor and gird his sword upon him. Each one shall mount his horse, and each shall set his stork upon his hand, and we will rise up and sight against the city, opposite to the place of the serpents."

> When they came to the appointed spot, the king said to them, "Let each man send forth his young stork, to descend upon the serpents." Thus they did, and the birds swooped down and devoured all the reptiles and destroyed them. After the serpents were removed in this way, the men fought against the city, subdued it, and killed all its inhabitants, but of the people besieging it there died not one.[34]

The themes of birds – primarily eagles – killing snakes has been exhaustively treated by Rudolf Wittkower in his article "Eagle and Serpent," in his *Allegory and Migration of Symbols*, New York, 1997, pp. 15–44, showing the global range of this motif. But for our purposes we shall call attention to the Hindu myth concerning the mighty sun-god eagle, Garuda. And so it is related in Vettam Mani's *Puranic Encyclopaedia*, Delhi, 1975, p. 282 (s.v. Garuda 7):

> Garuḍa approached the pot of nectar,[35] and Viśvakarmā who attacked him first was felled to the ground. The dust storm raised by the waving of Garuḍa's wings blinded everybody. The Devas and Indra, nay, even the sun and the Moon lined up against Garuḍa, but he defeated them all, and entered the particular place where the pot of nectar was kept. Two terrific wheels were rotating round the pot and they would cut into mince-meat anybody who tried to lay hands on the pot and a machine circled the wheels. Below the wheels were two monstrous serpents with glowing eyes and protruding tongues like flashes of fire, and the serpents never closed their eyes. The very look with those eyes was enough to poison anyone to death. Garuḍa blinded those

34. See "*Divrei ha-Yamim shel Moshe Rabbenu alav ha-Shalom*," apud. A. Jellineck, *Beit ha-Midrash*, vol. 2, second ed., Jerusalem, 1938, pp. 6–7; *Sefer ha-Yashar*, ed. Venice, 1624, *Exodus* 133b–136b; Yalkut Shimoni 1, *Exodus* 168; etc.; Ginzberg, *Legends*, vol. 5, Philadelphia, PA, 1925, pp. 407–408, note 80. He also refers us to Josephus, *Antiquities* 2:10–11, line 246, Loeb ed., vol. 1, p. 271, where birds are ibes rather than storks.

35. *Amrtakalaśāparanam* (the pot of nectar carried away).

> eyes by raising a torrent of dust, pierced them in the middle with his beak and through the hole, his body reduced to such a tiny shape, went nearer to the pot. He destroyed the wheels and the machine, and carrying the pot of nectar in his beaks rose to the sky shielding the light of the sun by his outspread wings. Mahāviṣṇu, who became so much pleased with the tremendous achievements of Garuḍa asked him to choose any boon. Garuḍa requested Viṣṇu that he should be made his (Viṣṇu's) vehicle and rendered immortal without his tasting amṛta. Both the boons were granted.

Wittkower further relates this motif to the "Roc" theme, ibid., pp. 94–95, relating it to "the fight between the Indian solar bird Garuda and the chthonic snake Naga," mentioned in the two great Sanskrit epics *Mahabharata* 1:1353, and the *Ramayana* 3:39, referring also to A. de Gubernatis, *Zoological Mythology*, vol. 2, London, 1872, p. 94.[36] In the Jewish version of this popular myth it is the stork *Hassidah* (feminine) from *Hasid*, a righteous one who has supplanted the eagle in her virtuous act.[37]

36. And in Wittkower, ibid., pp. 38–39, yet other species of birds appear in place of the classic eagle, e.g., the ichneumon, and a swan-like avian creature, etc.

37. It may well be that the stork came to replace the eagle in this legend because of the stork's love of water (see de Gubernatis, ibid., p. 261), while the serpent is frequently an aquatic creature in world mythology (ibid., pp. 388–420). And see further ibid., pp. 180–206.

18. The Stick That Turned into a Serpent

The author of *Indica*, Albiruni (c. 1030 C.E.) tells the following tale (ed. Sachau, Lahore, 1962, vol. 1, p. 156):

> Another story of theirs is the following: – Brahman had a son called Narada, who had no other desire but that of seeing the Lord. It was his custom, when he walked about, to hold a stick. If he threw it down, it became a serpent, and he was able to do miracles with it. He never went without it. One day being engrossed in meditation on the object of his hopes, he saw a fire from afar. He went towards it, and then a voice spoke to him out of the fire: "What you demand and wish is impossible. You cannot see me save thus." When he looked in that direction, he saw a fiery appearance in something like human shape. Henceforward it has been the custom to erect idols of certain shapes.

Cf. editor's note, vol. 2, p. 400, that this story "is not known to me from other sources." Of course, the editor recognized the similarity to the Moses story in *Exodus* 7:10–15, where Moses' staff is turned into a serpent (*nahash*).

19. Splitting Seas and Rivers

Exodus 14:26–31 which describes the splitting of the Red Sea – really Reed Sea, Hebrew: *Suf* – and the passage of the people of Israel through it, is discussed in detail by J. G. Frazer in his *Folk-Lore in the Old Testament: Studies in Comparative Religious Law*, vol. 2, London, 1918, pp. 456– 462. This theme, found in many other cultural milieux, finds a partial parallel in a legend of the Balija of India, cited by E. Thurston in his *Castes and Tribes of Southern India*, vol. 1, Madras, 1909, p. 139, which reads as follows:

> The Kāpus and Balijas, molested by the Muhammadan invaders on the north of the northern Pennār, migrated to the south when the Pennār was in full flood. Being unable to cross the river, they involved their deity to make a passage for them, for which it demanded the sacrifice of a first-born child. While they stood at a loss what to do, the Mālas who followed them boldly offered one of their children to the goddess. Immediately the river divided before them, and the Kāpus and the Balijas crossed it, and were saved from the tyranny of the Muhammadans. Ever since that time, the Mālas have been respected by the Kāpus and Balijas, and the latter even deposited the images of Gauri, the bull and Ganesa, which they worshipped, in the house of a Māla.

See further Thurston, vol. 5, pp. 74–75 (Morasu caste):

> .... Their flight soon came to the ears of the chief, who, being vexed and mortified at the trick they had played on him, set out with his attendants like a raging lion in quest of his prey. The fugitives at length came to the banks of the Tungabhadra river, which they found full and impassable, and their cruel pursuer nigh at hand. In the dreadful dilemma, they addressed to the God Vishnu the following prayer. 'O! Venkatrāma (a title of Vishnu), if thou wilt graciously deign to enable us to ford this river, and wilt condescend to assist us in crossing the water, as thou didst Hanumant in passing over the vast ocean, we from henceforth will adopt thee and thy Hanumant our tutelary deities.' Vishnu was pleased to grant their prayer, and by his command the water in an instant divided, and left a dry space, over which they passed. The moment they reached the opposite bank, the waters closed and prevented their adversary from pursuing them, who returned to his own country. The sect settled in the provinces near the Tungabhadra river, and in course of time spread over the districts which now form the eastern part of the kingdom of Mysore then called Morsu, and from thence arose their surname."

For further parallels, see Theodor H. Gaster, *Myth, Legend, and Custom in the Old Testament*, vol. 1, Gloucester, MA, 1975, pp. 237–240, note 86, and p. 386; idem, *Passover: Its History and Traditions*, New York, 1949, pp. 42–45.

20. Moses and the Footprint of God

Anyone who goes to Varanasi, that magical place of myth and mystery, where past and present meet, will go to see the "footsteps of Visnu" set in marble at the Manikarmika ghat. Hardwar also has such a footprint inset in stone in the upper wall of Har-Ki-Sauri. It is said to be that of Lord Visnu and the waters of the Ganga touch it at all times. However, the phenomenon of sacred footprints is found not merely in Varanasi. See, e,g,, W. Crooke, *Things Indian*, London, 1906, pp. 231–232, who wrote:

> The myth of the footprints stamped on the rock by gods and mighty men is found in all parts of the world....
>
> The most celebrated of these marks is that at the summit of Adam's Peak in Ceylon, a hollow 5 feet long and 2½ wide, which Buddhists venerate as the mark of the Master; Saivites as that of Siva, Musalmans as that of Father Adam. One of the most sacred Hindu marks of this kind is the Vishnupada, or footmark of Vishnu, at Gaya in Bengal, which is preserved in a silver basin under a canopy and within a shrine. But all sorts of deities, saints, holy animals like the cow, heroes like the Mahratta Sivaji, are commemorated in this way all over India.
>
> The Muhammadans have appropriated the idea, and revere in many places the Qadam-i-Rasul, or footprint of the Prophet. One of these was brought from Mecca by a pilgrim in the days of Akbar, who ordered the grandees of the Court to meet it and

> carry it themselves by turns. But he paid no particular respect to the relic, and allowed the discoverers to keep it in their own house.

See also W. Crooke, *The Popular Religion and Folk-Lore of Northern India*, London, 1896, vol. 2, p. 199, and accompanying illustration.

Ibn Batuta in his *Travels* (ed. Tim Mackintosh, London, 2002, p. 248) mentions:

> The blessed Footprint of our father – Adam … on the lofty black rock in a wide plateau. The blessed Foot sank into the rock far enough to leave its impression hollowed out. It is eleven spans long. In the rock where the Foot is there are nine holes cut out, in which infidel pilgrims place offerings of gold, rubies and pearls. You can see faqirs, after they reach the cave of al-Khidr, racing one another from there to take what is in these holes.

Crooke continues:

> The Indian fancy for exalting their deities by portraying them of monstrous size is shown in the dimensions of some of these relics. The Chinese pilgrim, Hiuen Tsiang, saw a footprint of the Budda in the Deer-park at Benares which was 500 feet long. Their love of symbolism is shown in the emblems which they carve upon it – in Tibet, the Eight Glorious Marks – the golden fish, umbrella, victorious banner, vase, lotus, and wheel. The Burmese make it nearly square, with the toes all of the same length, and divide the sole into 108 squares, in which they represent all sorts of things – monasteries, tigers, fish, priests, and the like – signifying that all these things are under the feet of the Master.

He is referring to the mountain called Sarandib (7,357 feet in height). Adam is supposed to have descended on it when expelled from Paradise. Hence, it is called "Adam's Peak." See also *The Travels of Ibn*

Batuta in the Near East, Asia and Africa, ed. Samuel Lee, London, 1829, pp. 30, 185, 190.

See the note of the edition of *The History of Marco Polo*, eds. Yule-Cordier, New York, 1993, vol. 2, pp. 320–321:

> "The Dewa of Samantakúta (Adam's Peak), Samana, having heard of the arrival of Buddha (in Lanka or Ceylon) ... presented a request that he would leave an impression of his foot upon the mountain of which he was guardian.... In the midst of the assembled Dewas, Buddha, looking towards the East, made the impression of his foot, in length three inches less than the cubit of the carpenter; and the impression remained as a seal to show that Lanka is the inheritance of Buddha, and that his religion will here flourish." (*Hardy's Manual*, p. 212.)
>
> [Ma-Huan says (p. 212): "On landing (at Ceylon), there is to be seen on the shining rock at the base of the cliff, an impress of a foot two or more feet in length. The legend attached to it is, that it is the imprint of Shâkyamuni's foot, made when he landed at this place, coming from the Ts'ui-lan (Nicobar) Islands. There is a little water in the hollow of the imprint of this foot, which never evaporates. People dip their hands in it and wash their faces, and rub their eyes with it, saying: "This is Buddha's water, which will make us pure and clean.'" – H. C.]
>
> "The veneration with which this majestic mountain has been regarded for ages, took its rise in all probability amongst the aborigines of Ceylon.... In a later age, ... the hollow in the lofty rock that crowns the summit was said by the Brahmans to be the footstep of Siva, by the Buddhists of Buddha, ... by the Gnostics of Ieu, by the Mahometans of Adam, whilst the Portuguese authorities were divided between the conflicting claims of St. Thomas and the eunuch of Candace, Queen of Ethiopia." (*Tennent*, II. 133.)
>
> ["Near to the King's residence there is a lofty mountain reaching to the skies. On the top of this mountain there is the impress of a man's foot, which is sunk two feet deep in the rock,

> and is some eight or more feet long. This is said to be the impress of the foot of the ancestor of mankind, a Holy man called *A-tan*, otherwise P'an-Ku." (*Ma-Huan*, p. 213.) – H. C.]
>
> It is a perplexing circumstance that there is a double set of indications about the footmark. The Ceylon traditions, quoted above from Hardy, call its length 3 inches less than a carpenter's cubit. Modern observers estimate it at 5 feet or 5½ feet. Hardy accounts for this by supposing that the original footmark was destroyed in the end of the sixteenth century. But Ibn Batuta, in the 14th, states it at 11 spans, or *more* than the modern report. [Ibn Khordâdhbeh at 70 cubits. – H. C.] Marignolli, on the other hand, says that he measured it and found it to be 2½ palms, or about half a Prague ell, which corresponds in a general way with Hardy's tradition. Valentyn calls it 1½ ell in length; Knox says 2 feet; Herman Bree (De Bry?), quoted by Fabricius, 8½ spans; a Chinese account, quoted below, 8 feet. These discrepancies remind one of the ancient Buddhist belief regarding such footmarks, that they seemed greater or smaller in proportion to the faith of the visitor! (See *Koeppen*, I. 529, and *Beal's Fah-hian*, p. 27.)

For a similar description by John De' Marignolli, 1290–c.1328, apud *Cathay and the Way Thither*, by H. Yule and H. Cordier, vol. 3, London, 1916, pp. 227, 233, and notes ad loc.

Hardwar also has such a footprint inset in stone in the upper wall of Har-Ki-Pauri. It is said to be that of Lord Vishnu, and the waters of the Holy Gorge touch it at all times.

However, what for me is most intriguing is what I found in several early rabbinic texts relating to *Exodus* 17:6. There Moses is told by God:

> Behold, I will stand before thee there upon the rock (*ha-tzur*) in Horev.

And the Sages expounded that He said to him:

> Every place that you find the impression or imprint of my foot, there I [will be] before you.

See *Tanhuma be-Shalah* 25; *Mechilta* to *Exodus*, ibid; *Masechta* 4, *Parasha* 6, ed. Ish Shalom 52b, and *Targum Yonatan* to *Exodus*, ibid., where however he has "imprints of a foot," without "my." And in *Mechilta de-Rashbi*, eds. Epstein and Melamed, Jerusalem, 1955, p. 118, line 21, the reading is "the imprint of a human foot, as it is written, as the likeness of a man" (*Ezekiel* 1:26) – clearly an explanatory expansion.

The commentators explain that *ha-tzur*, the rock, is homiletically interpreted as deriving from *tzurah*, a form, hence "*roshem*" = impression, imprint. Louis Ginzberg, in his *The Legends of the Jews*, vol. 5, Philadelphia, 1928, pp. 20–21, note 122, rightly calls this a "strange statement," suggesting that it "is very likely the oldest reference to the religious significance of the dolmens, whose form is described here as being similar to that of the human foot (toes?)". But this seems somewhat far-fetched. Could this be some sort of reference to the Indian notion of a deity's footprint in stone?

Here we may add that which I came across in A. M. T. Jackson and R. E. Enthoven, *Folk Lore Notes I: Gujarat*, Bombay, 1914, p. 92:

> When an *atit* or holy man or a recluse dies, his body is interred, and a platform rising waist high from the ground, or a small dome-shaped temple, is built over the spot. This is called a samadh. An image of the god Shiva is generally installed in the samadh; but sometimes padukas i.e. *the impressions on stone of the footsteps of the deceased*, are installed instead. Instances of the latter are the padukas of Dattatraya, Gorakha and Machchendra Nath. [My emphasis – D. S.]

And cf. ibid., p. 114:

> Most high caste people, on the deaths of their first wives, take an impression of their feet on gold leaves or leaf-like tablets

> of gold and cause the second wives to wear them around their necks. These impresses of feet are called *shok–pagalars* or mourning footprints.

But this may have a different explanation, namely that these imprints will prevent the deceased wife from causing injury to the second wife (ibid., p. 115).

Finally, when recently in Sikkim I visited the Kecheodpari Lake (elevation 6,400 feet), close to the road between Yuksam (or Yoksum) and Gwalching, which originally was called *Kha-Chot-Parli*, one of the myths associated with the lake is that it should be associated with the footprint of the Hindu god, Lord Shiva, who is said to have meditated in the Dupukney Cave high above the lake. A plaque at the entrance to the Lake gives the basic information. From a high overlook its contours appear to be in the shape of a footprint.

Crooke did not mention this particular example.

It is perhaps of interest to note that in Scotland:

> The Stone of Scone is a relic of the ancient belief that a sacred stone conveys power and that an oath taken upon it has a peculiar sanctity. The Lords of the Isles, at their installation, *stood upon a stone with footmarks cut out in it*, thus denoting that they would walk in the footsteps of their predecessors in uprightness and in loyalty to the Clan, and the inauguration of a Chief took place 'at the Stone', the 'sacred place' associated by long tradition with the ceremony, in the presence of the assembled tribe or clan. [My emphasis – D. S.]

See F. Marian McNeill, *The Silver Bough*, vol. 1, Edinburgh, 1956, p. 90.

21. The Scapegoat

In *Genesis* 16:22, we read of the ritual of the scapegoat:

> And the goat shall bear upon him all their iniquities unto the land which is cut off; and he shall let go the goat in the wilderness.

Edgar Thornton (and K. Rangachari) in *Castes and Tribes of Southern India*, vol. 1, Madras, 1909, p. 112, writes, when describing the funeral rites of the Bagadas of the Nilgiris, in Tamil Nadu, as follows:

> Then a buffalo calf was led twice around the bier, and the dead man laid on its head by this act, the calf was supposed to receive all the sins of the deceased. It was then driven away to a great distance, that it might contaminate no one, and it was said that it would never be sold, but looked on as a dedicated animal.

This was already noted by James G. Frazer, in *Anthologia Athropologia: The Native Races of Europe and Asia*, London, 1939, p. 230, quoting Thurston, "Anthropology," *Madras Government Museum Bulletin*, 2/4, Madras, 1899, p. 4.

22. Cities of Refuge

In *Numbers* 35:9 et seq. we learn of the cities of refuge wherein anyone who has killed another by accident may seek refuge, and be safe from the hand of the avenger of blood.

Ibn Batuta, who visited South India and the Malabar region in the early fourteenth century, writes as follows:

> In the country of Malabar are twelve kings, the greatest of whom has fifty thousand troops at his command; the least, five thousand or thereabouts. That which separates the district of one king from another, is a wooden gate upon which is written: "The gates of safety of such are one." For when any criminal escapes from the district of one king, and gets safely into that of another, he is quite safe; so that no one has the least desire to take him, so long as he remains there.

See *The Travels of Ibn Batuta in the Near East, Asia and Africa 1325–1354*, ed. Samuel Lee, London, 1829, p. 167. The editor, ad loc., notes that "this custom seems nearly allied to that which obtained among the Israelites…"

23. Never-Ending Oil

Russell, ibid., vol. 4, p. 557, section on the *Teli,* relates as follows:

> Similarly the temple of Vishnu at Rājim is said to be named after one Rājan Telin, who discovered the image lying abandoned by the roadside. She placed her skin of oil on it to rest herself and on that day *her oil never decreased,* and when she had finished selling in the market she had all her oil as well as the money. Her husband suspected her of evil practices, but, when next day her mother-in-law laid a skinful of oil on the image and the same thing happened, it was seen that the god had made himself manifest to her, and a temple was built and named after her and the image enshrined in it.

A similar theme is familiar to us from the story of Elisha and the Shunamite woman in 2 *Kings* 4:3–5, where from a single cruse of oil she filled up numerous empty vessels which she borrowed from her neighbors. Gaster (ibid., vol. 2, pp. 518–519, 560), brings a number of parallels from diverse sources, noting the famous [classical] story of Philemon and Baucis who entertain Jupiter and Mercury out of their scant store, only to discover to their amazement that "every time the wine bowl is emptied, it fills up again of its own accord." He goes on to attempt to trace the theme to early Canaanite theological texts, but this part of his argument is somewhat forced.

A similar motif may be found in Edgar Thurston's *Castes and Tribes of Southern India*, vol. 4, Madras, 1909, pp. 306–307, s.v. Mādiga, where he relates the following version of the story of Ellammā, the goddess for all people, and the cause of the universe:

> She is said to have proceeded on a certain day to the town of Oragallu, accompanied by Jana Mātangi. On the way thither, the soles of Mātangi's feet blistered, and she sat down with Ellammā beneath a margosa tree. After resting a short time Mātangi asked Ellammā's permission to go to a neighbouring Īdiga (Telugu toddy-drawer), and get some toddy to drink. Ellammā objected, as the Īdiga Gauda was a Lingāyat, and Mātangi would be compelled to wear the lingam. When Mātangi persisted, Ellammā transformed herself into an ant-hill, and Mātangi, in the guise of a young woman, went to the Īdiga Gauda with her cane (Jogi kolu) and basket, and asked for toddy. The Gauda became angry, and, tying her to a date-palm (*Phoenix sylvestris*), beat her, and gave her cane and basket to his groom. Mātangi was further ill-treated by the Gauda and his wives, but escaped, and went to the Gauda's brother, who treated her kindly, and offered her toddy, of which he had sixty loads on bullocks. All this he poured into the shell of a margosa fruit which Mātangi held in her hand, and yet it was not filled. Eventually the toddy extracted from a few palms was brought, and the shell became full. So pleased was Mātangi with the Īdiga's treatment of her, that she blessed him, and instructed him to leave three date-palms untapped as Basavi trees in every grove.

24. Cure of Leprosy and Leprosy as a Punishment

RUSSELL, IBID., VOL. 3, p. 183 (*Malba* caste):

> The story continues that the reason why the Halbas came to settle in Bastar and Kānker was that they had accompanied one of the Rājas of Jagannāth in Orissa, who was afflicted with leprosy, to the Sihāwa jungles, where he proposed to pass the rest of his life in retirement. On a certain day the Rāja went out hunting with his dogs, one of which was quite white. This dog jumped into a spring of water and came out with his white skin changed to copper red. The Rāja, observing this miracle, bathed in the spring himself and was cured of his leprosy.

We are reminded of the biblical tale in 2 *Kings* 5, where Naaman, captain of the host of the King of Syria, who was afflicted with leprosy, at the advice of Elisha bathes seven times in the river Jordan (verse 14) "and his flesh came again like unto the flesh of a little child, and he was clean." See further Gaster, ibid., vol. 2, pp. 519–520 on the motif of "Bathing cures leprosy."

We may further add that the motif of leprosy as a punishment, as in *Numbers* 12:10, where Miriam is punished by becoming leprous for speaking badly of Moses' wife, is paralleled in Indian thought, as noted by Verrier Elman in his *Myths of Middle India*, Madras, 1949, p. 347, note 2, with bibliographic references.

25. The Judgment of Solomon

Strictly speaking, this is not an Indian legend but a Tibetan one. But its similarity to the well-known judgment of Solomon tale in 1 *Kings* 3:16–28 is sufficiently striking to merit its inclusion in this selection. I came across it in A. L. Shelton's *Tibetan Folk Tales*, New Delhi, 2008, pp. 164–165:

> Once upon a time two women were quarrelling over one boy, trying to decide to which one he belonged. They could not settle the case, so they took it before the king of the land, who, being wise and of great understanding, thus ordered: "One of you take hold of the right hand of the boy and the other of the left hand and pull, the one who gets him may carry him off."
>
> When he had so spoken, she, who was not the boy's mother, because she had no love for him, and not caring whether she hurt him or not, pulled with all the force she had. She, who in truth was the boy's mother, because she loved him, and fearing she might hurt him, though she was the stronger of the two, did not pull very hard. Them the king said to her who had pulled very hard, "He is not your son, but belongs to the other woman," to whom he gave the boy, who at once happily carried him away.

A similar variation on this theme may be found in J. A. B. Buitenen, *Tales of Ancient India*, Chicago and London, 1959, pp. 168–169, in a tale entitled "Mahosadha's Judgement" ("Comm. On Mahāummāga Jātaka," Fausböll, II, 336:31, 337:15, see Buitenen ibid., p. 260). See further W. R. S. Ralston and Anton von Schiefner, *Tibetan Tales Derived from Indian Sources*, London (n.d., 1906), pp. XLIII and 120–123.

I also found a parallel in Jan de Vries, *Volksverhalen uit Oost-Indië*, Thieme & Cie, Zutphen, vol. 2, 1928, pp. 32, 393. According to this version, a demoness had stolen a child in order to eat it. The mother and the demoness come before the sage, who rules that the child be cut in half. The true mother offers to give the child to the other mother as long as it is left alive. At which the sage perceives that since no two persons ever look alike, one of them must be a demon, and the one willing to give up the child as long as it is left alive, must be the real mother. See also Jan Knappert, *Mythology and Folklore in South-East Asia*, Oxford, 1999, pp. 301–302, and ibid., cf. pp. 165–166 in the Cambodian version of "the Bodhisattva as Solomon."

For additional examples of this motif, see Theodor H. Gaster, *Myth, Legend, and Custom in the Old Testament*, New York and Evanston, 1969, section 150, pp. 491–494, 551, with rich bibliographic references.

26. Creating an Alternative Cosmos

In the *Yalkut Shimoni Ezekiel*, section 359, we find a long passage describing how Hiram the king of Tyre created an alternative cosmos. I quote here Louis Ginzberg's rewording in his *The Legends of the Jews*, vol. 4, Philadelphia, 1913, pp. 335–336:

> Hiram, the king of Tyre, was a contemporary of Nebuchadnezzar, and in many respects resembled him. He, too, esteemed himself a god, and sought to make men believe in his divinity by the artificial heavens he fashioned for himself. In the sea he erected four iron pillars, on which he built up seven heavens, each five hundred ells larger than the one below. The first was a plate of glass of five hundred square ells, and the second a plate of iron of a thousand square ells. The third, of lead, and separated from the second by canals, contained huge round boulders, which produced the sound of thunder on the iron. The fourth heaven was of brass, the fifth of copper, the sixth of silver, and the seventh of gold, all separated from each other by canals. In the seventh, thirty-five hundred ells in extent, he had diamonds and pearls, which he manipulated so as to produce the effect of flashes and sheets of lightning, while the stones below imitated the growling of the thunder.
>
> As Hiram was thus floating above the earth, in his vain imagination deeming himself superior to the rest of men, he suddenly perceived the prophet Ezekiel next to himself. He had

> been waved thither by a wind. Frightened and amazed, Hiram asked the prophet how he had risen to his heights. The answer was: "God brought me here, and He bade me ask thee why thou art so proud, thou born of woman?" The king of Tyre relied defiantly: "I am not one born of woman; I live forever, and as God resides on the sea, so do I."
>
> Hiram's palace was swallowed up by the earth, and in the bowels of the earth it will remain until it shall emerge in the future world as the habitation of the pious.[38]

In the *Ramáyana* 59:20, transl. Robert P. Goldman, New York University Press, 2005, vol. 1, p. 309, we read as follows:

> Then standing among the seers, besides himself in rage, the renowned and mighty sage [Vishva-mistra] created a whole new set of constellations in the south like a second Brahma, lord of creatures, creating another "Seven Seers" in the southern portion of the sky. When he had created this new set of constellations, he spoke, choking with rage, "I will create another India, or perhaps the world should be without an India." And in his wrath he began to create even gods. At this the bulls among the gods and the host of seers became thoroughly alarmed and spoke soothing words to the great Vishva-mitra: "Illustrious ascetic;

38. See Ginzberg's notes in vol. 6, pp. 424–426, note 105. It is interesting to note that among the Hassidim of Tsanz it was the practice not to make a blessing on hearing thunder, in contradiction to the established custom to do so. See *Shulhan Aruch Orah Hayyim* 227:1 based on *Mishnah Berachot* 6:1. And the blessing is either "...whose strength and might fill the world," or "... who carries out the works of creation" (*Baer Heiteiv* ad loc.). A similar testimony as to this negative practice is to be found in *Siftei Hachamim* to *Megillah* 6a, apud R. Moshe Reischer's *Shaarei Yerushalayim* (*Shaar ha-Gevul*), Jerusalem, 1967 (written in 1862), that in Safed, on hearing thunder they do not make a blessing, *saying that it maybe came from Hiram's seven heavens*. Similarly, in R. Hayyim ha-Levi Horowitz' *Hibat Yerushalayim*, Jerusalem, 1844 (Hof ha-Yam 18, s.v. Tzar), etc. See in detail Avraham Benyamin Meir Boim, "*Birkat ha-Raamim ve-ha-Berakim*," *Tsanz* 506, 2020, pp. 8–12.

> this king [Tri-charka] has been owned by his *guru*'s curse, he is not worthy of bodily entering heaven..."

And in another version of this legend we are told that Brihaspati – a Rishi sage, guru of all Devas, sometimes identified with Agni – ordered him to stop ... In the process of creating this alternative universe all the *tapas* that he had gained from his very severe austerities were used up, and he had to start all over again to achieve the status of Brahmarshi and to become an equal of Vashista.

(See *Ramayana*, ed. Rajagopalachari, Bombay, 1958, p. 19.)

There is here a thematic similarity to the Jewish Kabbalistic notion that the ascetic can spend many years trying to ascend to the spiritual heights of *gadlut ha-mochin*, but as soon as he arrives, he immediately plunges down back to *katnut ha-mochin*.

And compare the tale told of Reb Baruch of Mezbizh (died 1811), related in Martin Buber's *Tales of the Hasidim*, New York, 1975, Book I, p. 92:

The Fiftieth Gate

> Without telling his teacher anything of what he was doing, a disciple of Rabbi Baruch's had inquired into the nature of God, and in his thinking had penetrated further and further until he was tangled in doubts, and what had been certain up to this time, became uncertain. When Rabbi Baruch noticed that the younger man no longer came to him as usual, he went to the city where he lived, entered his room unexpectedly, and said to him: "I know what is hidden in your heart. You have passed through the fifty gates of reason. You begin with a question and think, and think up an answer – and the first gate opens, and to a new question! And again you plumb it, find the solution, fling open the second gate – and look into a new question. On and on like this, deeper and deeper, until you have forced open the fiftieth gate. There you stare at a question whose answer no man has ever found, for if there were one who knew it, there

would no longer be freedom of choice. But if you dare to probe still further, you plunge into the abyss." "So I should go back all the way, to the very beginning?" cried the disciple.

"If you turn, you will not be going back," said Rabbi Baruch. "You will be standing beyond the last gate: you will stand in faith."

Part II

Rabbinic Parallels

27. Omen: The Rooster That Crows at Night

In my *The Jewish Life Cycle*, vol. 2 [hereafter *JLC*, vol. 2], planned for publication in 2025, chapter 27, I discuss the evil omen of the rooster that crows at night citing *B. Shabbat* 67b, and that should this happen and one slaughtered it as a consequence, this would be considered a forbidden act as it follows the "Amorite practice." In Russell, ibid., vol. 4, p. 105, in Mandla, among the Gonds, "if a cock crows at night, a man will get up at once, catch it and twist its neck, and throw it over the house as far as he can. Apparently the cock is supposed to be calling to the evil spirits. If a hen cackles, or lays eggs at night, it is considered inauspicious, and the bird is often killed or given away." This latter is also mentioned in *B. Shabbat*, ibid., and discussed at length in my *The Jewish Life Cycle*, vol. 1 [hereafter *JLC*, vol. 1], Oxford Ramat-Gan, 2008, pp. 359–372.

28. Saints in the Fiery Furnace

R. C. Temple, *The Legends of the Panjab*, vol. 3, London, 1893, No. XLVII, "The Saints of Jálandhar," (VIII), p. 195, which tells of the miracle of Sayyid 'Abdulla, called the Tanûri of Jálandhar, who Nawāb Tughlaq of Lahore (fourteenth century CE) threw into a hot oven …

The tyrant gave an order: "Quickly heat the oven.
And let this Sayyid have a good taste of his brethren!"
Said the Sayyid: "I make no complaint; the will of God
I take upon me without hesitation; this (duty) is above all."
When the iron of the oven was thoroughly red hot,
The Sayyid, saying "In the name of God," entered into it.
As soon as the Sayyid had entered the oven
The royal servants quickly shut down the lid.
On the third day (afterwards) that evil tyrant sent an official
To bring him the Saint's ashes without any delay.
The royal servant went and lifted up the lid.
He found the Saint repeating the Creed inside it!
Said he: "0 Saint, come out of it now!"
Said (the Saint): "Never mind, send the Governor to me."
When the Governor heard of this he came quickly on foot.
And was anxious to be forgiven….

Cf. *Daniel* 3:19–30

Then was Nebuchadnezzar filled with fury, and the form of his visage was changed against Shadrach, Meshach, and Abed-nego; he spoke and commanded that they heat the furnace seven times more than it was wont to be heated. And he commanded certain mighty men that were in his army to bind Shadrach, Meshach, and Abed-nego, and to cast them into the burning furnace. Then these men were bound in their cloaks, their tunics, and their robes, and their other garments, and were cast into the midst of the burning furnace. Therefore because the king's commandment was peremptory, and the furnace exceeding hot, the flame of the fire slew those men that took up Shadrach, Meshach, and Abed-nego. And those three men, Shadrach, Meshach, and Abed-nego, fell down bound into the midst of the burning fiery furnace.

Then Nebuchadnezzar the king was alarmed and rose up in haste; he spoke and said to his ministers: "Did not we cast three men bound into the midst of the fire?" They answered and said unto the king: "True, O King." He answered and said: "Lo, I see four men loose, walking in the midst of the fire, and they have no hurt; and the appearance of the fourth is like a son of the gods." Then Nebuchadnezzar came near the mouth of the burning fiery furnace; he spoke and said: "Shadrach, Meshach, and Abed-nego, ye servants of God Most High, come forth, and come hither." Then Shadrach, Meshach, and Abed-nego came forth out of the midst of the fire and the satraps, the prefects, and the governors, and the king's ministers, being gathered together, saw these men, that the fire had no power upon their bodies, nor was the hair of their head singed, neither were their cloaks changed, nor had the smell of fire passed on them. … Then the king promoted Shadrach, Meshach, and Abed-nego in the province of Babylon .

For the later versions of the legend, see Louis Ginzberg, *Legends of the Jews*, vol. 6, Philadelphia, 1928, pp. 416–419, notes 85–90.

And for partial parallels to the Jonah story, see Temple, ibid., vol.

2, pp. XVI, 505, vol. 3, p. 498; and see above in the Introduction similarity to Potiphar's wife, see ibid., vol. 2, pp. 396 et seq. As to boring a servant's ear, see vol. 1, pp. 2, 329–330, 332, and J. G. Frazer, *Folk-Lore in the Old Testament*, London, 1918, vol. 3, chapter 3, pp. 165–269. These are motifs that require further examination.

29. Sneezing as an Omen

In *JLC*, vol. 1, pp. 389–390, 403–407, I discussed at length the various aspects of sneezing as an omen, usually of a coming disaster, a death or suchlike, citing numerous sources from a diversity of cultures. Russell, ibid., vol. 4, p. 585, relates that among the *Thugs*:

> If any member of the party sneezed on setting out on an expedition or on a day's march, it was a bad omen and required expiatory sacrifices; and if they had travellers with them when this omen occurred, these must be allowed to escape and could not be put to death.

See further W. Crooke, *The Popular Religion and Folk-Lore of Northern India*, London, 1896, vol. 1, pp. 240–241, on this subject; and Enthoven, *Folklore of Gujarat*, London, 1914, pp. 113–114.

30. A Knife in the Bed of a Woman in Childbirth

In *JLC*, vol. 1, p. 361, we cited rabbinic sources (such as *T. Shabbat* 6:4 and 6:13) which advise the use of iron in the bed of a woman in childbirth as a form of protection. And cf. ibid., pp. 26–27, note 21, for additional sources. And in my *Minhagei Yisrael*, vol. 6, p. 53, note 14, I pointed to the use of the sword behind the woman's bed as a form of protection; cf. ibid., vol. 1, p. 233, and vol. 8, p. 26, note 23, etc.

Enthoven, in his *Folklore of Konkan*, London, 1915, chapter 5 (at note 603), writes:

> A knife or another sharp weapon is kept under the bed of the woman [in childbirth] that the mother and her child may not be attacked by a spirit.

31. *Kapparot*

The *kapparot* ceremony on the eve of Yom Kippur is very familiar, in which a cock (for a male) or a hen (for a female) is waved three times above one's head and a prayer is annunciated, namely, that this cock or hen "may go to purgatory, while I will go forward to a good life." This is a form of the scapegoat motif, which I discussed in my *Minhagei Yisrael*, vol. 1, Jerusalem, 1989, pp. 33–34, vol. 3, p. 134, vol. 7, pp. 254, 349, and vol. 8, p. 256.

It is, therefore, interesting to read the following from R. E. Enthoven's *Folklore Notes*, vol. 2, *Folklore of Konkan*, Bombay, 1915, chapter 3 (at note 84):

> In the Málwah taluka of the Ratnágiris area, the scapegoat (often a cock) *is waved three times* round a sick person and thrown into the street. The man who goes to throw it away is prohibited from looking back. [My emphasis – D. S.]

There is a great deal of material on the scapegoat, much of which was collected in J. G. Frazer's magnificent *The Golden Bough* part IV, entitled "The Scapegoat," London, 1914 (and cf. ibid., p. 191). As to looking back, cf. above, section 8.

32. Drinking the Water in Which Feet Were Washed

In *JLC*, vol. 2, chapter 1, we mentioned an interesting tradition from the Jews of Kurdistan which Tamar (in *Alei Tamar*, vol. 1, Givatayim, 1979, p. 349) found in the travelogue of Benyamin ha-Sheni (*Masaot Benyamin ha-Sheni*, Lyck 1859), chapter 13 (p. 40). There he relates that:

> When a Jew comes to them from Jerusalem [a very rare event], then they all go to welcome him, and they kiss his shoulders, his beard, and also his feet, in accordance with his status and honour, and afterwards they bear him on their shoulders to the house of the Nasi, then they remove his shoes and wash his feet, and the water used for washing [his feet] they place in a utensil with sacred excitement. [I am in no way exaggerating (when I tell you that)]. And the notables of the congregation drink (of it), and what remains is for the women and children to drink, for they firmly believe [a futile belief] that these waters will protect those that partake of them from any disease and evil occurrence.

We may compare this with Russell, ibid., vol. 4, p. 70, where, if delivery of a baby is retarded, the mother:

> may be given water to drink in which the feet of her husband or her mother-in-law or a young unmarried girl have been dipped...

33. On Throwing Rice at a Wedding

In *JLC*, vol. 1, pp. 287–291, we discussed the practice of throwing confetti at weddings, pointing out that Jewish sources speak primarily of wheat kernels and similar such seeds. We noted that this was a widespread custom found among many cultures, with a number of variations. In vol. 2, chapter 23, subsections "On Throwing Rice or Grains at the Bride," I expanded on this subject showing that in many areas rice was thrown, noting that among the Bene Israel of N.W. India this was the practice (citing H. S. Keminkar, *The History of the Bene-Israel of India*, Tel-Aviv, 1937, p. 147), and this then is also the case for Hindus in Northern India (see W. Crooke, *Religion and Folklore of Northern India*, New Delhi, 1925, p. 293 and ibid., note 5). Indeed, this was a widespread practice in India; see R. E. Enthoven, *Tribes and Castes of Bombay*, vol. 1, Bombay, 1920, p. 57, etc.

34. Encircling as Part of the Wedding Ceremony

In *JLC*, vol. 1, p. 127, I discussed the custom of the bride encircling the groom three or seven times, and in vol. 2, chapter 14, I brought a number of parallels from diverse sources.

Throughout India we find the theme of seven times encirclement usually around a wedding pole. See, e.g., Russell, ibid., vol. 3, p. 76, among the Gonds, where the marriage post is made of the wood of the *mahua* tree, or among the Kurusi (vol. 4, p. 65), where the couple walk seven times around the marriage-post in the direction of the sun, and among numerous other customs, ibid., vol. 4, p. 590, vol. 3, p. 29, *Ghasia* caste; p. 191, *Halba*; p. 286, *Kachhi*; p. 442, *Khangār*; p. 489, *Kirār*; p. 535, *Koli*; p. 558, *Korku*, etc. And also cf. p. 460, *Khatri*. And vol. 4, p. 33, *Kumbi*; p. 65, *Kurni*; p. 152, *Majwar*; p. 327, *Panva* (to which we may add that the couple's skirts are tied together, cf. *JLC*, vol. 1, pp. 203–204, note 18, and *JLC*, vol. 2, chapter 20, on the *dextrarum iunctio*); p. 361, of seven times around *tanda* mats, *Pandhi*; p. 383, seven times around a well, *Parsi*; p. 407, seven times around the *chawk Rajjhar*; p. 420, *Rajput*.

See also W. Crooke and R. E. Enthoven, *Religion and Folklore of Northern India*, New Delhi, 1925, p. 339; idem, *Folklore Notes*, vol. 1; *Folklore of Gujaarat*, vol. 2, Bombay 1914, pp. 11–12; *Folklore of Konkan*, Bombay, 1915, chapter 5; idem, *Tribes and Castes of Bombay*, vol. 1, Bombay, 1920, p. 30, the Ahir, etc.

35. Stepping on the Foot at a Wedding

In *JLC*, vol. 1, p. 128, note 7, and in the *Addenda*, p. 702, I discussed in detail the Jewish custom of the groom's placing his right leg over the bride's left leg during the marriage ceremony, to demonstrate symbolically that he shall rule her all his life, noting other methods whereby the groom seeks to dominate his bride, or *vice versa.*

In Russell, ibid., vol. 2, London, 1916, p. 492, we read:

> Afterwards, the pair are seated in a marriage-shed, the bridegroom's leg being placed over that of the bride, with their feet in a brass dish....

And ibid., vol. 4, p. 134 (*Mahār* caste):

> The bridegroom presses his toe on the bride's foot....

Ibid., p. 343 (*Karan* caste):

> Each places the right foot on the left foot of the other and holds the other's ear with the hand....

And in vol. 3, p. 75 (*Gond* caste):

> Often the bride resists and the bridegroom has to force her fist

> open, or he plants his foot on hers in order to control her while he gets the ring onto her finger.

And in Edgar Thurston's *Castes and Tribes of Southern India*, vol. 1, Madras, 1909, p. 143, the Balija bridegroom also places his right foot on that of the bride; and ibid., vol. 3, p. 237 (the *Kapu* caste), where the bridegroom places his right foot on the left foot of the bride.

Cf. Russell, vol. 4, p. 355 (*Pardhān* caste):

> He tries to open her fist which she keeps closed, and when he succeeds in this he places an iron ring on her little finger and puts his right toe over that of the girl's…

On the ring motif, which is so common we make no comment, and on tying the ends of their clothes together see *JLC*, vol. 1, pp. 203–204, note 18, *JLC*, vol. 2, chapter 36, on the *dextrarum iunctio*, and above section 32 on Encircling as Part of the Wedding Ceremony.

36. Carrying the Bride Across the Threshold

In my *JLC*, vol. 2, pp. 300 et seq., I discuss the Jewish custom of the bridegroom's carrying the bride across the threshold of their new home. We had already referred briefly to this subject in *JLC*, vol. 1, p. 267, note 7, and considerably expanded on it in vol. 2, showing the wide dissemination of this practice in a variety of cultures.

An early testimony of this practice in mediaeval Ashkenaz may be found in *Sefer Gematriyot* by R. Yehudah he-Hassid, the author of *Sefer Hassidim* (died 1217), ed. Yaakov Stal, vol. 1, Jerusalem, 2005, pp. 308–310, section 287, who writes as follows:

> And it was the custom that when the bride first enters the house [of the bridegroom], while they lead her with torches and by candlelight on the morning of Friday, that the bridegroom lifts her up as she enters the house, in accordance with that which is written in 2 *Chronicles* 24:2, "And Yehoiada [literally] lifted up for himself (i.e., took to wife) two wives; one after the other", and it is written "and they [literally] lifted (i.e., took) their wives (Ruth 1:4), and a found object is acquired by being picked up (=lifted), and it is written "Who findeth a wife findeth a good thing" (*Proverbs* 18:22)....

This passage bases itself on the recurrent use of the root *naso*, to lift (also bears the semantic meaning of "to take to wife"), suggesting associatively that the act of marriage is like an act of conveyance (*hagbahah*). (See editor's detailed comments ad loc., and note 74, that the usual verb used for marrying is *lakahat*, as opposed to *va-yisa*).

Interestingly enough, J. G. Frazer, in his *Folk-Lore in the Old Testament*, vol. 3, London 1918, p. 8, tells us that "in ancient India it was the rule that the bride should cross the threshold of her husband's house with her right foot foremost, but should not stand on the threshold." And in ibid., note 2, he lists as his sources:

> The *Grihya-Sûtras*, translated by H. Oldenberg, part II, Oxford 1892, pp. 193, 263 (*The Sacred Books of the East*, vol. xxx); M. Winternotz, *Das altindische Hochzeitsrituell nach dem Wissenschaften in Wien*, Philosoph-Historrische Classe, xl.

See the rest of the discussion and the variety of these customs in *JLC*, ibid., passim.

37. The Status of the Broom

In *JLC*, vol. 1, p. 282, note 2, and again in *Addenda*, p. 723, I discussed the strange custom of dancing with a broom at the marriage of the youngest son in the family – the *mezhinik* in Yiddish; and there I brought similar related practices in our cultural milieux. This strange practice seems to have a parallel in Indian society, for Enthoven, in his *Folklore of Gujarat*, p. 149, relates that the broom is worshipped during the marriage, and there he gives additional aspects of the broom's "divinity." See also W. Crooke, *The Popular Religion and Folk-Lore of Northern India*, London, 1896, vol. 2, pp. 190–191.

38. The Navel Cord for a Barren Woman

In *JLC*, vol. 1, pp. 16–17, we commented on the practice of drinking bloody water… in order to gain fertility, and on swallowing menstrual blood. (And cf. ibid., p. 453.)

To this we may compare what E. S. Hartland, in his *Primitive Paternity*, vol. 1, London, 1909, p. 70, mentions that "other women, especially Jewesses, are said to suck blood from the child's navel, and in doing so they should swallow three times" (R. Kobert, *Historische Studien aus dem Pharmakologischen Institute de Kaiserlichen Universität, Dorpat*, vol. iv, Halle a S. 1894, p. 92). And ibid., p. 71, that "among the Ottoman Jews a woman who has only one child, and has afterwards ceased to bear, may recover her fertility by eating the foreskin removed from a child by circumcision" (*Mélusine* viii, p. 270).

We may further add that Russell, ibid., vol. 3, p. 88, when discussing the Gonds, states that:

> It is believed that if a barren woman can get hold of … another woman's child's … navel cord, she can transfer the mother's fertility to herself….

See also Enthoven, *Folklore of Gujarat*, p. 99, that barren women seek to eat the navel-string of a newborn baby, and cf. ibid., p. 99.

39. A Morbid Cure for Barrenness

In *JLC*, vol. 1, p. 452, we noted the Libyan Jewish and Muslim custom for barren women to drink the water in which a corpse was washed, and that they shriek above the body of a person who had been beheaded, and in Syria they were counseled to stand under a hanged man. See further *Addenda et Corrigenda*, pp. 749–750 on this issue.

Now we may add W. Crooke, in his *The Popular Religion and Folk-Lore of Northern India*, London 1896, vol. 1, p. 226, who mentions that barren women in India bathe underneath a person who has been hanged, "and women of the middle classes try to obtain a piece of wood of the gallows for the same object." He adds:

> Recently at an execution in Bombay, the hangman was observed to carefully secure the rope, and particularly that part of it which had encircled the neck of the culprit. He stated that he could sell each quarter inch of it, as it averted evil spirits and ghosts, and even prevented death from hanging....

Presumably barrenness was also caused by these malevolent spirits.

In *Addenda et Corrigenda*, ibid., I sought to explain this phenomenon as follows:

> We mentioned that in India barren women bathe under a hanged man. In order fully to understand this, one must know

that there is an ancient Indian doctrine that punishment atones, and blots out any guilt and reproach. This notion is discussed in Johann Jakob Meyer's *Sexual Life in Ancient India* (Delhi, 1971), p. 394. I will cite his discussion verbatim:

> [This doctrine] is probably connected on the other hand with the teaching of the old verse which I quoted in that note to the *Daçakum,* and which, for instance, is also found in Vasishtha, xix, 45; Manu, viii, 318; Nārada, Pariçishta, 48: The criminal punished by the king goes without a spot into heaven, like the pious man. Cp. *My Hindu Tales,* pp. 9–10 [note]. In Sicily, too, as I point out in the *Daçakum [âracaritam,* Leipzig, 1902] executed criminals are prayed to and worshipped. Cp. E. S. Hartland, "The Cult of Executed Criminals at Palermo," *Folk-Lore,* vol. 21, p. 168 ff.; ibid., vol. 7, p. 275; *idem Primitive Paternity,* London 1909, I, 77. And in general anyone meeting his end by violence is outside the course of nature, and becomes a god, an evil spirit, etc. "There is a deified Pootra in every Rajput family – one who has met with a violent death." J. Tod, *Rajasthan,* London 1829, I, 298, note; cp. 659-60; E. S. Hartland [*Primitive Paternity*] I, 77; *idem Zschr. D. Ver. f Volksk.,* Bd. 2, p. 185; *Zschr. f Religwissensch,* Bd. 8, p. 258. Much valuable information is given especially by W. Crooke, *The Popular Religion [and Folklore of Northern India,* Westminster 1896], I, 43, 44, 46, 62, 96, 99,115, 119, 129, 138 ff., 147, 189 ff., 230 f., 234 ff.; Crooke, *The North-Western Provinces* [of *India,* London, 1897], 252.

However, this notion gained widespread currency, and, as indicated above, made its way into the Mediterranean areas and other parts of Europe, as well as the Middle East. Cf. also George Henderson, *Survivals in Belief among the Celts* (Glasgow, 1911), p. 305.

What is surely a related belief is that which is found in

Cuddesden in Oxfordshire, cited in *Choice Notes from "Notes and Queries": Folklore* (London, 1859), p. 258, namely that "stroking the swollen neck with the dead hand of a man who had been hanged" was a remedy for a goiter (I), and cf. ibid., p. 10.

40. Cutting off the Nose of an Adulterous Woman

The Rosh, in his responsa (*Klal* 18:13) relates the case of a Jewish woman who committed adultery with a non-Jew, and the court cut (off) her nose as a punishment, and "so that she should be repugnant to her adulterer," and this testimony is cited by the Rama in *Shulhan Aruch Even ha-Ezer* 177:5. However, *Besamim Rosh*, Bedin 1793, sect. 192, cites R. Shimshon be-R. Avraham who states this is unacceptable. And though *Besamim Rosh* is a forgery, here it reflects mainstream Jewish ethical thinking.

See R. V. Russell and Rai Bahadur Hīra Lal, *The Tribes and Castes of the Central Provinces of India*, 1916, vol. 4, p. 525, in the section on the *Sunār* caste, who write as follows:

> The *nathni* has some mysterious connection with woman's virtue, and to take off her nose-ring – *nathni utarna* – signifies to dishonour a woman.... In northern India women wear the nose-ring very large and sometimes cover it in *parda*. It is possible that the *practice of Hindu husbands of cutting off the nose of a woman detected in adultery* has some similar association, and is partly intended to prevent her from again wearing a nose-ring. [My emphasis – D. S.]

See also N. M. Penzer, *The Ocean of Story*, vol. 5, London, 1926, pp. 82, 156, on cutting off the nose and ears of a faithless wife. (The full title of this book is *The Ocean of Story, Being C. H. Tawney's Translation of Somadeva's Kathā Sarit Sagara (or Ocean of Streams of Story)*, now edited with introduction, fresh explanatory notes, and terminal essay by N. M. Penzer. I have shortened the title henceforth.)

41. How the Corpse Should Be Taken Out

In *JLC*, vol. 1, p. 437, note 11, we noted that the corpse should be placed on the ground with his feet towards the entrance, indicating that he is ready to go forth through the entrance to his final resting place.... In vol. 2, chapter 31, we cited *Tzavaat R. Yehudah he-Hassid* 10 (ed. Margaliot, Jerusalem, 2002, p. 13), that it should be taken out feet first, and there we brought additional evidence for this practice in other traditions.

W. Crooke, in his *Native Races of Northern India*, London, 1906, p. 217, writes:

> The corpse is laid upon a bier and carried away feet foremost as that the ghost may not find its way back into the house....

See also *JLC*, vol. 1, p. 467, note 7, and in J. G. Frazer's *The Fear of the Dead Returning in Primitive Religion*, vol. 3, London, 1936, pp. 30–31, and in my vol. 2, chapter 20, where we discuss this theme in detail.

42. Taking the Dead Out of the House

In Russell, ibid., vol. 3, p. 93, we read that among the Gonds:

> If one or two persons die in a house in one year, the family often leave it and make another house. On quitting the old house they knock a hole in the back wall to go out so as to avoid going out by the front door.

In *JLC*, vol. 2, chapter 31, I showed that in a variety of cultures the dead were taken out by a special opening such as a breach or a hole in the wall which afterwards was closed up. I noted that it was tantalizing to compare this phenomenon with what is alluded to in *B. Baba Batra* 12a and *Y. Avodah Zara* 3.9, 43b, where we learn of the "breaking open of doorframes" and opening up of walled entrances and resealing them (*paratz et pesimav*) to take out the dead body, and its influence on the status of the house vis-à-vis its impurity. Here it is the removal of the dead that is through a hole in the wall, while among the Gonds it is the owners of house that exit through such a break in the wall.

43. Impurity of the House in Which a Corpse Is to Be Found

Jewish sources both biblical and rabbinic deal as extensively in the laws and degrees of impurities as the result of contact direct or indirect with a corpse. Indeed, there are whole Tannaitic tractates dealing with the various aspects of this issue (in *Seder Taharot*), such as *Kelim* and *Oholot*. Vessels found in the house in which a dead body is present become impure and require purification through immersion in a *mikveh*. However, earthenware vessels cannot ever be purified, and they must be broken and thrown away.[39]

Enthoven, in his *Folklore of Konkan*, chapter 6 (at notes 692–694) writes as follows:

> Hindus believe that impurity attaches to all things in consequence of the death of a person in that house.

39. See what I wrote in my *Material Culture in Eretz-Israel during the Talmudic Period*, Jerusalem, 1993 [in Hebrew], p. 20, note 31, where I wrote:

> And so I saw when I was in India, that they sell cups (of tea) in earthenware vessels that have not been fired, and they are thrown away immediately after use.... And this is because of their rules of impurity....

I am referring to the fact that people of a lower caste would defile these vessels, and if another caste-member were to touch them, he would become impure.

See also David Adan-Bayewitz's comments, ibid., pp.178–183. And cf. below, p. 134, "that earthenware pots.... are all broken.... and cannot be purified by washing..."

> All things that can be purified by washing are washed and taken back, while things, like earthen pots, cooked food, etc., are thrown away. Special care is taken to break the pots, so that they may not be used again. Even the walls of the house are white-washed..... The mourners who use earthen vessels during the mourning period break them at the end of the mourning period.

To this we may add what W. Crooke wrote in his *Religion and Folklore of Northern India*, New Delhi, 1925, pp. 236–237:

> One way of barring the return of the ghost is to remove the corpse from the house by a special way or door, not generally used by inmates, and to close it after the funeral has started, so that the spirit may not be able to find its way back. This end is also attained by prohibiting the removal of the corpse by any but a single gate of the town or village, generally that facing south which leads it straight to the realm of Yama, but the primitive ritual ordained that the corpse of a Sūdra should be taken out by the southern gate, by the western if a Brahman, by the northern if a Kshatriya, and by the eastern if a Vaisya (S. Stevenson, *The Rites of the Twice-Born*, Oxford, 1920, p. 149; H. T. Colebrooke, *Essays on the Religion and Philosophy of the Hindus*, London, 1858, p. 98). Meitheis never remove the corpse from the house over the threshold of the main door, but cut a hole in the wall or use the tiny side entrance (T. C. Hudson, *The Meitheis*, London, 1908, p. 117). Maghs in Bengal, when the house-master has died, throw down the ladder leading up to the house, and the mourners on their return must effect an entrance by creeping through a hole in the back wall (H. H. Risley, *The Tribes and Castes in Bengal*, vol. 2, Calcutta, 1892, p. 34). The same precautions are used by Musalmāns. When a death occurs in one of the palaces of the Nawāb of Bahāwalpur the body is carried out through a hole in the wall; at Maler Kotla it used to be forbidden to bring a body into the town without special

permission, and then not by one of the gates, but through a hole broken in the town wall (H. A. Rose, *A Glossary of the Tribes and Castes of the Punjab and North Frontier Province*, vol. 1, Lahore, 1911, p. 869). It is a remarkable fact that the corpses of the Emperors Akbar and Shah Jahan were removed from the palace by a special way (V. A. Smith, *Akbar, the Great Mogul*, Oxford, 1919, p. 327; Manucci, *Storia do Mogor*, ed. W. Irvine, vol. 2, London 1908, pp. 126, 431; and cf. J. G. Frazer, *The Belief in Immortality*, London, 1918, pp. 452 et seq.). With the intention of facilitating the departure of the ghost the feet of the dying and the dead are turned in the direction of the house entrance, and with the object of baffling the ghost it is usual to carry the corpse feet foremost to burial or cremation, and on the way the bearers halt and reverse the position (*The Bombay Gazeteer*, ed. J. M. Campbell, vol. 9/1, Bombay, 1883, p. 48; S. Stevenson, *the Rites of the Twice-Born*, Oxford, 1920, p. 149).

44. Passing under the Bier or Palanquin[40] of a Corpse

In *JLC*, vol. 1, pp. 451–452, I discussed the Eastern Jewish custom of walking under the bier, thus:

> When a man dies and leaves a pregnant woman [in Libya] it is customary for the bearers of the bier to stand with the bier at the entrance of the room from which the corpse was taken out, and the widow passes under the bier, in the view of the congregation of those escorting [the funeral procession].

And in Baghdad, to ensure the fertility of women, a bride would go to the corpse after it had been washed and walk three or four times above it, so that she would conceive.

Enthoven, in *Folklore of Gujarat*, p. 99, relates that a means of assuring conception is to pass under the bier of a corpse of a holy man, or an ascetic, while it is being carried to the country.

See further *JLC*, vol. 1, p. 452, that barren women would bathe under a hanged man and the explanation given in *Addenda*, pp. 748–750, by J. J. Meyer in his *Sexual Life in Ancient India*, Delhi, 1971, p. 391.

---

40. The word is derived from Sanskrit *paryaṅka* or *palyaṅka*, a bed, from which we have Hindi *palki*, Telluga *pallakī*, Pali *pallanko*, a couch bed or litter, Japanese *palangki*, litter, or sedan. The nasal termination in *palankeen* or *palanquin* comes from Portuguese. See in detail in Henry Yule and A. C. Burnell, *Hobson-Jobson: The Anglo-Indian Dictionary*, 1886, pp. 658–661, s.v. Palankeen.

45. Direction in Which the Bodies Are Buried

In *JLC*, vol. 1, pp. 519–523, and in vol. 2, chapter 36, section on "Grave Orientations," I discuss the different views on how the body should be oriented in the grave, citing, *inter alia* (1, p. 523), the *Magen Avraham, Orah Hayyim* 3:7, who comments that R. Menachem Azariah de Fano ruled in accordance with the *Zohar* (*Ba-Midbar* 118b) that when sleeping the head should be to the west and the feet to the east. This, indeed, was also the orientation of Jewish graves in Eppingen, Germany. See R. Bischoff and R. Hanke, *Die Judische Friedhof im Eppingen*, Eppingen, 1996.

Among the *Gadba* caste, "the dead are buried with the feet to the west, ready to start for the region of the setting sun" (Russell, ibid., 3, p. 12). So too the Gonds (ibid., p. 89), etc.

46. Deceased Is Buried Lying on His Side

In *JLC*, vol. 1, pp. 506–508, we discussed the ruling that a corpse can be buried "on his back, with his face upwards" (*Shulhan Aruch, Yoreh Deah* 362:2), or lying on his side (*Beur ha-Gra*, ibid., subparagraph 4). I showed that though this was an accepted practice, it was actually based on a misinterpretation of a passage in *Yerushalmi Ketubot* 12:3, as revealed by S. H. Kook (*Studies and Researches*, Jerusalem, 1967, p. 100, Hebrew) in the name of S. Lieberman.

Nonetheless, I found it interesting to see that Edgar Thurston, in his *Castes and Tribes of Southern India*, vol. 1, Madras, 1909, p. 262, reports of the Bonthuks, that "the dead are usually buried, lying on the left side."

47. Covering Mirrors

In *JLC*, vol. 1, p. 438, note 4, and p. 57, note 26, and in *Addenda et Corrigenda*, pp. 739–740, I discussed at length the practice of covering mirrors during periods of mourning, and offered a conjectural reason therefore.

Likewise in Russell, ibid., vol. 1, 1916, p. 122, we read about the superstition of looking in a mirror, especially after dark, or seeing one's reflection in water.

48. Breaking Pots in the House of the Deceased

In *JLC*, vol. 1, pp. 581–582, note 55, I cited the practice of breaking a small water-filled clay vessel placed on a table near the corpse, and also that the beadle of the burial society breaks a pottery vessel on the threshold of the house proclaiming, "By the ban of Joshua son of Nun, that all his offspring shall not follow his bier to accompany him until members of the society have returned from the cemetery, etc." Interestingly enough, Jackson and Enthoven, in their *Folklore of Gujarat*, Bombay, 1914, p. 133, also record the practice of breaking an earthenware vessel in the house of the deceased, or at the village gate on the way back from the cemetery. Others place such vessels on the spot the corpse was laid in the house, and then they are broken at the village gate. Likewise Jackson and Enthoven in *Folklore of Konkan*, Bombay, 1915, p. 66, write that "earthenware pots that are required for the funeral rites of the dead are all broken," and so too pots found in the house of the dead cannot be purified by washing but have to be broken, so that they may not be used again. Also idem, *Folklore of Gujarat*, p. 132.

See also E. Thurston, *Castes and Tribes of Southern India*, vol. 5, p. 16, that at the funeral of the last Maratha King of Tanjore, Mahāraja Sivāji, in 1855, "a boy of twelve was carried thrice round the pile, and at the last circuit a pot of water was dashed to pieces on the ground."

49. Breaking Water-Filled Vessels at a Funeral

In *JLC*, vol. 1, pp. 581–582, I cited the following:

> It was the custom in our city [Aden] to turn the bed of the deceased mortal to the wall, to spread a sheet over it, and to place under it a burning lamp **on a pottery vessel** all three days. And on the third day, the lamp together with the vessel are smashed on the grave of the deceased. There is a support for this in the Midrash and in the *Zohar.*

And in the notes (54–55), I made the following comments:

> See *Genesis Rabbah* 100:7, p. 1290, that "mourning is at its most intense on the third day," and the passage from the *Yerushalmi Moed Katan* cited there. Albeck, *Genesis Rabbah*, 1. 4, prefers the version of the Yerushalmi that the mourning is most intense for all of the first three days, and not only on the third day, bringing further sources in support of his view. "And after three days the cup breaks by itself" (*Y. Moed Katan*, loc. cit), and then the soul departs. This apparently is the time to smash the lamp with its vessel, as if to release the soul. It should be noted that according to the Iranian religion, the "*urwan*," the parallel of the Jewish soul, passes over to the place of judgment, after having tarried in the vicinity of the body for three days. See W. W. Malandra,

An lntroduction to Ancient lranian Religion Minneapolis, 1983, p. I04.

As to the reference to the *Zohar*, it is to *Zohar Hayyei Sarah*. See Bergman, *Jewish Folklore*, Jerusalem, 1935, p. 18. The breaking of the vessel is reminiscent of the burial custom of Meshed Jewry, that after the washing of the corpse the rabbi of the congregation encircled the body seven times, with each circuit accompanied by the breaking of one of the small, water-filled clay vessels that were placed for this purpose on the table near the corpse (see above, beginning of chap. 15). Benayahu, *Studies in Memory of the Rishon Le-Zion R. Yitzhak Nissim*, pp. 179–80, quotes Abraham Moses Luncz, "Religiose und soziale Gebrauche der Israeliten im Heiligen Lande," *Jerusalem* (Vienna, 1882) (Hebrew); *Lu'ah Eretz Yisrael* 4, p. 21: "When the members of the [burial] society leave with the deceased from the entrance to his house, the beadle of the society breaks a pottery vessel on the threshold of the house, and proclaims: 'By the ban of Joshua son of Nun, that all his offspring shall not follow his bier to accompany him until the members of the society have returned from the cemetery.'" And following Luncz, Rabbi Isaac Alfayah also writes (*Kuntres ha-Yehieli*, "Cemetery," 8b): "A pottery vessel or shards of a pottery vessel are broken at the entrance to the house, on the outside, and the ban of Joshua son of Nun is issued and decreed for all his offspring, that they are not permitted to follow his bier." It would seem, therefore, that this breaking of the pottery vessel is a part of the "ban" ceremony, possibly similar to "the inflated skin-bottles that are broken during the ban ceremony" (*Arukh ha-Shalem*, s.v. "*Heset*", vol. 5, p. 229a).

Similar customs are also to be found among non-Jews, albeit for different reasons. See, e.g., Westermarck, *Ritual and Belief in Morocco*, London, 1926, vol. 2, p. 481, that in Mequinez in North Africa, the Muslims place jugs filled with water on the grave, so that the deceased will be able to slake their thirst at the time of their resurrection.

E. Thurston, in *Castes and Tribes of South India*, vol. 5, p. 41, records the practice of the Haravan caste as follows:

> .... The karma karta (chief mourner) walks thrice round the corpse, carrying an earthen vessel filled with water, in which two or three holes are pierced. He allows some water to fall on the corpse, and breaks the pot near the head, which lies to the south. No Brāhman attends this part of the ceremony. When he has broken the pot, the karma karta must not see the corpse again; he goes away at once, and is completely shaved.

A similar practice is found among the Nayar, as recorded by Thurston, ibid., pp. 352, 361; the Okkiliyan, ibid., p. 442; and the Palan, ibid., p. 484; and cf. ibid., vol. 6, p. 185, among the Pattanavan caste; and cf. ibid., p. 246 (Rāvula caste).

50. Marriage of the Dead[41]

Here we will call attention to the somewhat macabre practice described in Moshe Klein's *Minhagei Hatunah etzel ha-Am ha-Yehudi le-Eidotav* (Wedding Customs among the Jews in the Various Communities), Israel, 1994, p. 115. He begins by quoting a Ukrainian author, Czerpiak Kareni. who wrote a book on the Marriage of the Dead (Chaskov 1930) [a book I have not seen], where, *inter alia*, he relates that if a bride or bridegroom die before their wedding, they carry out a marriage ceremony for them. The bride is dressed up in her wedding gown, and/or the groom has a hat with a garland of flowers. Similarly, Klein tells us, is the case in France, citing a French newspaper from August 30, 1960, which gives two descriptions of dead people's weddings in France. In one case, a young lady of 21, named Reymunde Suri, was to get married on May 21, 1960, to a policeman, Jean Farashi, who was killed on May 4, 1960, by Algerian terrorists. The wedding took place in a hall in the city of Melun on August 29. The hall was decorated with flowers which were brought by the bride's relatives and friends of the dead policeman. The bride sat in a "wedding throne" dressed as a mourner, with her parents and witnesses next to her. The mayor of the city gave the official permission for the wedding to take place, so that she be married to the deceased. She

41. I discuss this in detail in my *JLC*, vol. 2, chapter 24, and here I am highlighting Indian material, which there I did not cite in full.

was asked if she agreed to this and answered positively, after which the mayor shook her hand and called her Madame Farashi. The ceremony ended, and they all went on to the cemetery to place a wreath on the grave.

He then describes a second such event, at the special order of General de Gaulle, etc. He ends by stating that this practice is to be found among a number of different religious communities, and most usually among Jews the wedding takes place in a cemetery with a black *huppah* (canopy) in privacy, or in the dead person's house.

And on p. 114, he writes that if a bride died close to her wedding. it was the custom in Ashkenazi communities to place a black *huppah* over her bier, a black cloth supported on four poles, in the cemetery, with candles lit by her side. The groom places the wedding ring that he had prepared next to her and, as it were, marries her. This custom was abolished, but is referred to in *Masechet Semachot* 8:2, ed. M. Higger, New York, 1931, p. 149 (English translation and Commentary by Dov Zlotnick, New Haven and London, 1966), p. 57:

> A canopy should be made for the "bride" and the "groom" from which both that is fit and that which is unfit for food may be suspended.

Zlotnick discusses this passage (ibid., pp. 14–15), rejecting those scholars who interpreted it as referring to a live bride and groom (G. Aton), arguing persuasively that it refers to dead ones, and showing that this is how it was understood by medieval commentators. We shall not repeat his arguments, only to point out that an inscription from the Necropolis of Marissa on a gold leaf which reads "Good luck to the bridal" *(eutuchos tois numphiois),* and which has a number of small holes suggests that it "was stitched on the clothing of a dead person, who was thus facilitated on the bridal with death." The editor adds a note that "a custom of bridal with death is still observed in Palestine in connection with the bridal of unmarried persons of marriageable age."[42] That there exist parallels in other cultural milieux bears out this understanding of the *Semachot* text. So, for instance, we read in Tekla Domötör's *Hungarian Folk Customs*, Hungary, 1988, p. 63:

> The custom of holding a ceremonial wedding on the death of a young man or girl was still practiced in most parts of the country at the tum of the century. The mourners used to dress in festive clothes on these occasions and walk in procession to the grave. The fiancé, lover or occasionally a relative, acted as "bride" or "bridegroom" to the deceased and were given a present by the family in reward for their pain. The deceased boy was accompanied by bridesmaids and the girl by best men.

We may add the following description is found in Tekla Domötör, *Hungarian Folk Beliefs* (original title: A magyar nép hiedclemvilága, Corvina 1981, transl. M. Mann), Budapest, 1982, pp. 257–258:

> Celebrating "the dead person's wedding" was also customary in Hungary. When the deceased had not yet reached adulthood he or she would be buried with all the splendour of the wedding, accompanied by bridesmen or bridesmaids. The ceremony is still performed in some areas even today, with the role of the bride or groom being taken by a girl or a young man who knew the deceased...
>
> Scholars formerly believed this to be a custom peculiar to Hungary, but this is not the case; ceremonial weddings for the deceased are practiced by other peoples scattered throughout both Europe and Asia.

And perhaps (indirectly) related to the above is that which we read

42. See *The Hellenistic Paintings of Marisa* by David M. Jacobson, Maney, 2007, p. 73, inscription no. 33.

in W. Crooke, *Religion and Folklore of Northern India*, ed. R. E. Enthoven, New Delhi, 1925, p. 192:

> One of the usual modes of preventing the ghosts or childless ancestors and those who have met with a violent death from giving trouble is to present a cow to a Brahman. but, *particularly in southern India, there is the remarkable custom whereby the corpse of a bachelor is formally wedded to a living girl.* There seems to be no record of this rite in the north, and the revolting proceeding described by some writers seems to be based on a misunderstanding. [My emphasis – D. S.][43]

Here I should like to bring the material cited in E. Thurston's *Castes and Tribes of Southern India*, Madras, 1909, ibid., p. 250–251:

> In some cases, girls who have died unmarried are supposed to haunt the house, and bring trouble thereto, and they must be propitiated by marriage. The girl's relations go in search of a dead boy, and take from the house where he is a quarter of an anna, which is tied up between two spoons. The spoons are tied to the roof of the girl's house. This represents the betrothal ceremony. A day is fixed for the marriage, and, on the appointed day, two figures, representing the bride and bridegroom, are drawn on the floor, with the hands lying one on the other. A quarter-anna, black beads, bangles, and a nose-screw are placed on the hands, and water is poured on them. This is symbolical of the dhāre ceremony, and completes the marriage.

Ibid., vol. 3, p. 334:

> Concerning a form of marriage between the living and the

43. He refers us to the following sources: R. E. Enthoven, *Tribes and Castes of Bombay*, Bombay, 1920–1922, vol. 1, p. 14; J. A. Dubois, *Hindu Manners, Customs and Ceremonies*, Oxford, 1906, p. 16 et seq., etc.

dead, performed by members of this caste if a man and woman have been living together, and the man dies, Mr. Hutchinson writes as follows.[44] "The sad intelligence of her man's death is communicated to her neighbours, a guru or priest is summoned, and the ceremony takes place. According to a writer who once witnessed such a proceeding, the dead body of the man was placed against the outer wall of the verandah of the house in a sitting posture, attired like a bridegroom, and the face and hands besmeared with turmeric. The woman was clothed like a bride, and adorned with the usual tinsel ornament over the face, which, as well as the arms, was daubed over with yellow. She sat opposite the dead body, and spoke to it in light unmeaning words, and then chewed bits of dried cocoanuts and squirted them on the face of the dead man. This continued for hours, and not till near sunset was the ceremony brought to a close. Then the head of the corpse was bathed, and covered with a cloth of silk, the face rubbed over with some red powder, and betel leaves placed in the mouth. Now she might consider herself married, and the funeral procession started." This refers to the Vīra Saiva or Lingāyat Kōmatis of the Northern Circars.

Ibid., vol. 6, p. 22 (Pallion Vanuivan Caste):

> Men who die before they are married have to go through a *post-mortem* mock marriage ceremony. A garland of arka (*Calotropis gigantea*) flowers is placed round the neck of the corpse, and mud from a gutter shaped into cakes, which, like the cakes at a real marriage, are placed on various parts of the body.

Ibid., pp. 111–112 (Paraiyan Caste):

> If the dead person is unmarried, a mock marriage ceremony, called kanni kaziththal (removing bachelorhood), is performed

44. *Marriage Customs in Many Lands*, 1897.

> before the corpse is laid on the bier. A garland of arka (*Calotropis gigantea*) flowers and leaves is placed round its neck, and balls of mud from a gutter are laid on the head, knees, and other parts of the body. In some places a variant of the ceremony consists in the erection of a mimic marriage booth which is covered with leaves of the arka plant, flowers of which are placed round the neck as a garland.

Vol. 1, p. 117:

> If a dead man leaves a widow in a state of pregnancy, who has not performed the *kanni kattodu* or marriage thread ceremony, this must be gone through before the corpse is taken to the pyre, in order to render the child legitimate. The pregnant woman is, at the time of the funeral, brought close to the cot, and a near relation of the deceased, taking up a cotton thread, twisted in the form of a necklace without any knots, throws it round her neck. Sometimes the hand of the corpse is lifted up with the thread, and made to place it round the neck. At the funeral of the young man, Mr. Clayton saw this ceremony performed on his pregnant wife. After a turmeric-dyed cord had been taken from the hands of the corpse and tied round her neck, she was again brought to the side of the bier, and her ear-rings, nose ornaments, and other articles of jewellery, were removed in token that she had become a widow.

In view of all of the above, perhaps this is not "based on a misunderstanding." Furthermore, Tekla Domötör's observation that "weddings for the deceased are practiced by other peoples scattered throughout both Europe and Asia" leads me to quote in full Henrie Cordier's note in his *Notes and Addenda to Sir Henry Yules edition...* of *Ser Marco Polo,* Paris, 1919 (included in the Dover edition of Yule-Cordier's *The Travels of Marco Polo*, vol. 2, New York, 1993, pp. 58–60):

> LV., p. 267. "They [the Tartars] have another notable custom, which is this. If any man have a daughter who dies before marriage, and another man have had a son also die before marriage, the parents of the two arrange a grand wedding between the dead lad and lass. And marry them they do, making a regular contract! And when the contract papers are made out they put them in the fire, in order (as they will have it) that the parties in the other world may know the fact, and so look on each other as man and wife. And the parents thence-forward consider themselves sib to each other, just as if their children had lived and married. Whatever may be agreed on between the parties as dowry, those who have to pay it cause to be painted on pieces of paper and then put these in the fire, saying that in that way the dead person will get all the real articles in the other world."

Kumagusu Minakata writes on the subject in *Nature,* Jan. 7, 1897, pp. 224–225:

> As it is not well known whether or not there is a record of this strange custom earlier than the beginning of the dynasty of Yuen, I was in doubt whether it was originally common to the Chinese and Tartars until I lately came across the following passage in *Tsoh-mung-luh* (Brit. Mus. Copy, 15297, *a* I, fol. 11–12), which would seem to decide the question – "In the North there is this custom. When a youth and a girl of marriage-able ages die before marriage, their families appoint a match-maker to negotiate their nuptials, whom they call 'Kwei-mei' (i.e., 'Match-Maker of Ghosts'). Either family hands over to a nother a paper noticing all pre-requisites concerning the affair; and by names of the parents of the intended couple asks a man to pray and divine; and if the presage tells that the union is a lucky one, clothes and ornaments are made for the deceased pair. Now the match-maker goes to the buryingground of the bridegroom, and, offering wine and fruits, requests the pair

to marry. There two seats are prepared on adjoining positions, either of which having behind it a small banner more than a foot long.

Before the ceremony is consecrated by libation, the two banners remain hanging perpendicularly and still; but when the libation is sprinkled and the deceased couple are requested to marry, the banners commence to gradually approach till they touch one another, which shows that they are both glad of the wedlock. However, when one of them dislikes another, it would happen that the banner representing the unwilling party does not move to approach the other banner. In case the couple should die too young to understand the matter, a dead man is appointed as a tutor to the male defunct, and some effigies are made to serve as the instructress and maids to the female defunct. The dead tutor thus nominated is informed of his appointment by a paper offered to him, on which are inscribed his name and age. After the consummation of the marriage the new consorts appear in dreams to their respective parentsin-law. Should this custom be discarded, the unhappy defuncts might do mischief to their negligent relatives... On every occasion of these nuptials both families give some presents to the match-maker ('Kwei- mei'), whose sole business is annually to inspect the newly-deceased couples around his village, and to arrange their weddings to earn his livelihood."

Kumagusa Minakata adds:

The passage is very interesting, for, besides giving us a faithful account of the particulars, which nowadays we fail to find elsewhere, it bears testimony to the Tartar, and not Chinese, origin of this practice. The author, Kang Yu-chi, describes himself to have visited his old home in northern China shortly after its subjugation by the Kin Tartars in 1126 A.D.; so there is no doubt that among many institutional novelties then introduced to China by the northern invaders, Marriage of the

Dead was so striking that the author did not hesitate to describe it tor the first time.

According to a Persian writer, after whom Pétis de Ia Croix writes, this custom was adopted by Jenghiz Kan as a means to preserve amity amongst his subjects, it forming the subject of Article XIX of his Yasa promulgated in 1205 A.D. The same writer adds: This custom is still in use amongst the Tartars at this day, but superstition has added more circumstances to it: they throw the contract of marriage into the fire after having drawn some figures on it to represent the persons pretended to be so marry'd, and some forms of beasts; and are persuaded that all this is carried by the smoke to their children, who thereupon marry in the other world (Pétis de la Croix, *Hist. Of Genghizcan,* trans. by P. Aubin, Lond., 1722, p. 86). As the Chinese author does not speak of the burning of papers in this connection, whereas the Persian writer speaks definitely of its having been added later, it seems that the marriage of the dead had been originally a Tartar custom, with which the wellknown Chinese paper-burning was amalgamated subsequently between the reigns of Genghiz and his grandson Kúblai – under the latter Marco witnessed the customs already mingled, still, perhaps, mainly prevailing amongst the Tartar descendants."

Yule himself, in vol. 1, p. 262, note 3, commented on this practice thus:

> This is a Chinese custom, though no doubt we may trust Marco for its being a Tartar one also. "In the province of Shansi they have a ridiculous custom, which is to marry dead folks to each other. F. Michael Trigault, a Jesuit, who lived several years in that province, told it us whilst we were in confinement. lt falls out that one man's son and another man's daughter die. Whilst the coffins are in the house (and they used to keep them two or three years, or longer) the parents agree to marry them; they send the usual presents, as if the pair were alive, with much ceremony

and music. After this they put the two coffins together, hold the wedding dinner in their presence, and, lastly, lay them together in one tomb. The parents, from this time forth, are looked on not merely as friends but as relatives – just as they would have been had their children been married when in life." (*Navarrete,* quoted by *Marsden.*) Kidd likewise, speaking of the Chinese custom of worshipping at the tombs of progenitors, says: "So strongly does veneration for this tribute after death prevail that parents, in order to secure the memorial of the sepulchre for a daughter who has died during her betrothal, give her in marriage after her decease to her intended husband, who receives with nuptial ceremonies at his own house a paper effigy made by her parents, and after he has burnt it, erects a tablet to her memory – an honour which usage forbids to be rendered to the memory of unmarried persons. The law seeks without effect to abolish this absurd custom." (*China,* etc., pp. 179–180.)

(Professor J. J. M. De Groot (*Religious System of China*) gives several instances of marriages after death; the following example (II. 804–805) will illustrate the custom: "An interesting account of the manner in which such *post-mortem* marriages were concluded at the period when the Sung Dynasty governed the Empire, is given by a contemporary work in the following words: 'In the northern parts of the Realm it is customary, when an unmarried youth and an unmarried girl breathe their last, that the two families each charge a match-maker to demand the other party in marriage. Such go-betweens are called match-makers for disembodied souls. They acquaint the two families with each other's circumstances, and then cast lots for the marriage by order of the parents on both sides. If they augur that the union will be a happy one (wedding) garments for the next world are cut out, and the matchmakers repair to the grave of the lad, there to set out wine and fruit for the consummation of the marriage. Two seats are placed side by side, and a small streamer is set up near each seat. If these streamers move a little after the libation has been performed, the souls are believed to approach each other; but if one of them does not move, the party represented thereby is considered to disapprove of the marriage. Each family has to reward its match-maker with a present of woven stuffs. Such go-betweens make a regular livelihood out of these proceedings.'"- H. C.)

The Ingushes of the Caucasus. according to Klaproth, have the same custom. "If a man's son dies, another who has lost his daughter goes to the father and says, 'Thy son will want a wife in the other world; I will give him my daughter; pay me the price of the bride.' Such a demand is never refused, even though the purchase of the bride amount to thirty cows." (*Travels, Eng. Trans.* 345.)

We may further note as a related example that in Tripoli the body of an unmarried woman is dressed as a bride when borne to the cemetery,[45] although this may be more closely related to the theme of

45. See E. Westermarck, *Ritual and Belief in Morocco*, London, 1926, vol. 2, p. 496. However, in faraway lndo-China, the Chins in the Minbu district continue the rites of marriage with the corpse if either of the contracting party dies. See *Gazetteer of Upper Burma and the Shan States*, Part 2, Rangoon, 1901, p. 302. And more disturbing is the practice in some centers in Southern India that if a girl having reached puberty dies unmarried, a man is hired for money to copulate with her, then, as it were, contracting for marriage. See J. B. Dubois, *Moeurs, lnstitutons et Ceremonies des Peuples de l'Inda*, 1862, vol. 1, p. 4. Although this is not really related to our subject, nonetheless it is interesting to call attention to yet another strange type of marriage, that is the marriage of two *sheidim* – demons. Max Grunwald, in his *Tales, Songs and Folkways of Sephardic Jews: Texts and Studies*, ed. Dov Noy [Hebrew], Jerusalem, 1982, p. 50, no. 25, tells us that, when the devils plan on having a celebration of dance for their marriage, they choose a house and demand of the owners to vacate it. They inform the owners of this by throwing stones into the house or wetting the walls. They turn over plates during meal-time, make the wine ferment in the goblets, until it bubbles over the rims. On Shabbat they throw small stones into the [oil] lamps so that they give little light. The owners will find their breakfast fried eggs thrown out to a cat or dog. They will continue to do all this until the owners comply with their demands. The house has to be in perfect order for their celebration, and if not, they are likely to break up everything in the house. See his additional comments on pp. 95–96, and p. 102 to no. 50, and pp. 106–107 to no. 59. There is a vast folkloric literature and research on the subject of demons, which we cannot deal with here. But one may be referred to Joshua

the similarity and relationship between marriage and death, a subject to which Shmuel Glick devoted a whole book: *Or Nogah Aleihem*, Efrat, 1977, *Light Has Dawned: The Relationship Between Marriage and Marriage Customs in Jewish Traditions* [Hebrew].

There are remnants of this practice in contemporary society, both in China ("ghost marriage") and in France since World War I (posthumous marriage), and more, but this goes beyond our purview.

And finally this practice is mentioned in *Shulhan Aruch*: *Yoreh Deah* 350, and the *Minhah Harevah*, by R. Pinhas Epstein, Jerusalem, 1923, to *Sotah* 12b, who found a source for this custom in that which is brought in *Sotah* ibid., namely that infant Moses' mother, when she placed him in the reed-basket, covered it in a *huppat neurim*, a canopy for the youth, saying to herself that perhaps she would not merit (i.e., live) to see his *huppah*, i.e., wedding. The Etz Yosef derived this midrashic statement from the verse in *Exodus* 2:6, where Pharaoh's daughter opens the basket and sees the child (*yeled*) "and behold it is a *naar* that is crying." Hence: *huppat neurim*.

Trachtenberg, *Jewish Magic and Superstition*, New York and Philadelphia, 1961, Index, s.v. Demons, on p. 339a.

51. Identifying Invisible Beings

In *B. Berachot* 6a, we are given a magical means to identify [evil] spirits. One of them is to take sifted ashes (*kitma nehila*) and presumably spread it on the ground, then go to bed, and in the morning you will see (the imprints of) cocks' feet. That is to say, although they are invisible, they will leave their footprints in the ashes. (See Louis Ginzberg, *The Legends of the Jews*, vol. 5, Philadelphia, 1925, p. 98, ibid., vol. 6, Philadelphia, 1928, p. 127, note 743.) Their feet apparently resemble those of a cock. (See also *Zohar* 3, 309a, Ginzberg, ibid., vol. 6, p. 301, note 92.) See also what I wrote in my *Minhagei Yisrael*, vol. 1, Jerusalem, 1989, pp. 127–131, with plentiful material on magical footprints in the dust.

Certainly Sanoi and Sansanos found in the famous amulet in *Sefer Raziel ha-Mal'ach* look like cocks. (See, e.g., my *Magic and Folklore in Rabbinic Literature*, Jerusalem and Ramat-Gan, 1994, p. 80, for illustration.)

A similar technique of catching invisible beings is found in Hemacandra's *The Lives of the Jain Elders*, transl. R. C. E. Fynes, Oxford New York, 1998, Canto 8 lines 396–400, p. 183:

> Cāṇakya said, 'Are you still so stupid that you've been letting yourself waste away for so long, like an ascetic who desires emancipation but does not know the truth?
>
> Never mind. You've done the right thing to tell me about it now. I'll soon catch the plunderer of your food.'

> After saying that, he sprinkled the floor of Candragupta's dining room with powdered clay, finer than barley meal.
>
> So when Candragupta sat down to eat, the footsteps of those two who had come to eat his food became visible on the powdered floor.

However, there were human beings who had made themselves invisible by magical means using a magic eye ointment. See continuation of this interesting tale. See also W. Crooke, *Native Races of Northern India* (*The Native Races of the British Empire*), London, 1906, p. 239, on spreading ashes on the floor of the hut to indicate footsteps of a spirit. And see W. Crooke, *Popular Religion and Folk-Lore in Northern India*, London, 1896, vol. 1, p. 176:

> After calling his father's spirit two or three times, the son returns to the house and examines the flour or ashes [that he spread on the tenth day after the death, a cubit square on the ground], and if the deceased did not die by the attack of a *Bhût*, the mark of his spirit is found on the flour or ashes in the shape of a footprint of a rat or a weasel.

And ibid., vol. 2, pp. 72–74:

> This use of ashes as a means of identifying the ghost constitutes in itself quite an important chapter in folk-lore: It reminds us of the Apocryphal legend of Bel and the Dragon. The idea probably originally arose from the respect paid to the ashes of the house fire by primitive races, among whom the hearth and the kitchen are the home of the household godlings.
>
> There are numerous instances of this practice from Europe. In the Western Islands of Scotland on Candlemas Day the mistress takes a sheaf of oats, dresses it in woman's apparel, and after patting it in a large basket beside which a wooden club is placed, cries three times, "Briid is come! Briid is welcome!" Next morning they look for the impression of Briid's club in

the ashes, which is an omen of a good harvest (T. F. T. Dyer, *Popular Customs*, London 1876, p. 57). Ash-riddled is a custom in the northern counties. The ashes being riddled or sifted on the hearth, if any one of the family be to die within the year, the mark of a shoe will be impressed upon the ashes (ibid., p. 199). In Wales they make a bonfire, and when it is extinguished each one throws a white stone into the ashes. In the morning they search out the stones, and if any one is found wanting, he that threw it will die within the year (ibid., p. 398). In Manxland the ashes are carefully swept to the open hearth and nicely flattened down by the women before they go to bed. In the morning they look for footmarks directed to the door, it means in the course of the year a death in the marriage (*Folk-Lore* 2, p. 310). According to one of the Italian charms, "And they were accustomed to divine sometimes with the ashes from the sacrifices. And to this day there is a trace of it, when that which is to be divined is written on the ashes with the finger or with the stick. Then the ashes are stirred by the fresh breeze, and one looks for the letters which they form by being moved" (G. G. Leland, *Etruscan Roman Remains in Popular Tradition*, London, 1892, p. 345).

Amongst some Hindus, on the tenth night after the death of a person, he who fired the funeral pyre is required to sift some ashes, near which a lamp is placed, and the whole covered with a basket. Next morning the ashes are examined, and the ghost is supposed to have migrated into the animal whose mark appears on the ashes (*North Indian Notes and Queries*, Allahabad, vol. 3, p. 35). So at the annual feast of the dead, the jungle tribes of Mirzapur spread ashes on the floor, *and a mark generally like that of a chicken's foot shows that the family ghosts have visited the house*. "On New Year's Eve," says Aubrey, "sift or smooth the ashes and leave it so when you go to bed; next morning look, and if you find there the likeness of a coffin, one will die; if a ring, one will be married" (W. Henderson, *Notes on the Folk-lore of the Northern Counties of England and the Border Folk-lore*

Society, London 1879, p. 57). In North Scotland, on the night after the funeral, bread and water are placed in the apartment where the body lay. The dead man was believed to return that night and partake of the food; unless this were done the spirits could not rest in the unseen world. This probably accounts for the so-called "food vases" and "drinking cups" found in the long barrows (W. Gregor, *Notes in the Folk-lore of the North-East of Scotland* [*Publications of the Folk-lore Society*], London 1881, p. 213). All Hindus believe that the ghosts of the dead return on the night or the Diwâlî or feast of lamps.

52. On Nail Pairings

W. Crooke, in his *The Popular Religion and Folk-Lore of Northern India*, Westminster (London), 1896, vol. 2, p. 278, informs us that:

> … natives of India are very careful about the disposal of hair-cuttings and nail-pairings….

And in his *Religion and Folklore of Northern India*, Oxford, 1925, p. 431, he writes:

> Hindus believe that the clippings of the hair and nails when buried in fertile ground will through the life immanent in them grow into a plant, and as the plant waxes in size it will absorb more and more of the owner's life, which will consequently wane and decline. Hence special care should be taken of such things.

He refers us to R. V. Russell, *The Tribes and Castes of the Central Provinces*, London, 1916, vol. 1, p. 102:

This we may compare with what we find in *B. Niddah* 17a:

> The Rabbis taught that three things have been said with regard to nail pairings: he who burns them is a *hassid* – a

> righteous man; he who buries them is a *tzaddik* – a pious man; he who throws them away is an evil man (*rasha*).

Rashi ad loc., explains that everything that comes from the human body can be injurious, citing the *Aruch* (s.v. *Shlosha*, *Aruch Completum*, ed. A. Kohut, vol. 8, pp. 90–95), which would suggest that one should do the same with hair-cuttings, as is done in the case of the Nazir (*Numbers* 6:18), who when ending his period of naziriteship burns his shorn hair. And cf. Ezekiel, chapter 5. And, indeed, there are Jewish sources that require shorn hair to be buried, or hidden (Rashi to *Ezekiel*, ibid., according to some readings).

In the later rabbinic sources there are different opinions as to whether the hair referred to comes from the head or the beard, and whether it is better to burn or to bury it. See in detail in R. Yaakov Hayyim Sofer, *Zechut Yitzchak*, vol. 2, Jerusalem, 1994, pp. 22–27, for a discussion of a wide variety of sources, but this is beyond the scope of this study.

53. Lice and Bugs

In the *Mahābhārata*, transl. J. A. B. van Buitenen, vol. 2, Chicago, 1973, 1(7) 84:10, p. 200, Yayati says that "Bugs [are] born from sweat..." And the translator, ibid., p. 453, note 10, explains that: there are four ways of being born, from a planet, from an egg, alive, or from sweat (insects)... Compare *B. Shabbat* 107b and ibid., 12a, from which it emerges (see Rashi, ibid., 12a, s.v. *Matirin*) that lice were spawned from man's flesh, perhaps meaning through the agency of sweat.

One of the corollaries of this view is that there is no prohibition to kill a louse on Shabbat (see *B. Shabbat* 12a, *Shulhan Aruch, Orah Hayyim* 316:9) since they are not born of a living creature. However, this assumption was based on the fact that in antiquity it was impossible to see the process of the birth and growth of minute creative with the basic eye. Only some three hundred years ago, when more sophisticated magnifying glasses were developed was it possible to discern such processes. Consequently, R. Yitzhak Lampronti (1679–1756) in his encyclopedic *Pahad Yitzhak* letter *Tzadi*, s.v. *Tzedah* (reprint Jerusalem, 1972) 21b, suggested that the halachah be changed, since now [in his day] scientific findings make it clear that they are born of living creatures, and hence it should be forbidden to kill them on Shabbat.

The argument continues among later authorities who do not wish to change the halachah despite scientific findings; see for a survey *Meorot ha-Daf ha-Yomi*, 1100, 2020, pp. 2–3; and see most recently the remarks of Michael Chernik, in his article "One Person's Science is Another's Superstition," *Conversations* 35, 2020, pp. 64–65.

54. Rivers Flowing Backwards

M. Gaster, in an article entitled "Some Ancient Oriental Folklore," in *Folklore*, London, 1938, p. 340, wrote:

> That rivers run backwards as the outward sign of a miracle is an idea familiar to classical structures from that beautiful chorus in the *Medea* of Euripides (410–411):
>
> > ... back flow the streams of the even – running river, Life,
> > Life is changed, and the laws of it are O'ertroal.

He also called our attention to the Roman poet Tibullus (1:2.44), and to the words of Cicero, *On Divination* 579a, suggesting that the source of the motif is Middle Eastern, referring us to *Psalms* 114:2, "... the Jordan turned backwards."

We may further add that in the famous story of *Tannur shel Ahnai* in *B. Baba Metzia* 49b, R. Eliezer told the other rabbis, "If the *halachah* (ruling) is according to me, let the waters of the channel prove it," and the waters of the channel turned backwards. (See my article "Zutot," in *JSIJ* 11, 2012, p. 9.)

Interestingly enough, Rabbenu Tam, in the *Tosafot* to *B. Shabbat* 65b, seeking to explain a difficult rabbinic text in the name of the mid-third century C.E. Babylonian authority, Rav, explains that:

> And therefore they – i.e. the Babylonians – knew when the rains came down in the Land of Israel, because the Euphrates [in Babylonia] turns round backwards (*she-hozer Prat le-ahorav*), because it is overflowing (*gedilato*) from the rains in the Land of Israel.
>
> (Parallels in *B. Nedarim* 40b, *B. Bechorot* 55b.)

There, then, we have a suggestion of a river turning its flow back upon itself regularly. The phenomenon of rivers turning backwards is known, but usually due to special circumstances, and not regularly. Thus, in 2012 the Amazon River flowed backwards after Hurricane Isaac. Similarly the Mississippi flowed backwards after that same hurricane. And at times geological factors can cause a change in the river's direction.

The same motif may be found in a Sikkimese legend concerning the river Teesta. For the Teesta (or Tista) River traverses Sikkim from North to South. Popular etymology derives its name from Nepali "*Thi-seesta-tha*" – "when did you arrive?", and local legends explain this on the basis of the legend relating to the meeting point of the Teesta and the great Rangit recorded in Vishay Doma's *Legends of the Lepchas: Folk Tales from Sikkim,* New Delhi, 2010, pp. 50–53:

> Teesta and Rangeet are two major rivers in Sikkim, both emanating from glaciers in the Sikkim Himalayas. Teesta resembles a young woman from the highlands as her sparkling water follows a straight path, traversing through lovely valleys and deep forests. The Rangeet meanders. Why do the two rivers take different paths from the Himalayas and why do they look different before they finally meet in the plains of Bengal and flow together for eternity?
>
> Many, many years ago, before the land of Sikkim was filled with people and when there were no monasteries, the river spirits Rangeet and Rongnyu, revered as Itbu-moo's [the Mother Creator] creations, were much acclaimed throughout the length and breadth of Mayel Lyang, not only for their matchless grace

and beauty but for their apparent love for one another They were never seen apart and went everywhere in each other's company.

The two river spirits used to meet secretly in a place high in the cloudcloaked, snow-shrouded lap of the Himalayas. But when their love was known to all, they offered salutations to Kongchen Kongchlo and decided to go away, very far, unseen by their friends. However, as if to conceal their sacred love, the river spirits decided to take different routes, promising to meet at Pozok. They issued a playful challenge to each other – their journey would be a race down to the distant plains.

Since the two spirits were venturing beyond the sacred environs of their home for the first time, they did not know the paths they were to travel. The lovers agreed to take a guide each on their long journey.

Being male, Rangeet was competitive, wanting to win against everybody, including his own lover. Rangeet chose tutfo, a mountain bird, to guide him to the plains. He knew the bird was the swiftest and would help him win the race. Rongnyu, was more subdued, older and pleasant. She decided to follow parilbu, a snake. Wishing each other well, as good friends do even when they are competing against each other, the river spirits set off.

The bird, while swift, would get distracted by the abundant fruit on the trees, the colourful flowers, or strange-looking insects. All these caught its fancy and it would wander off to play with other birds or to eat some fruit. Sometimes, it would rest awhile to enjoy the myriad colours or the forest. Rangeet followed the meandering, procrastinating tutfo, longing to meet Rongnyu, yet bound to his guide. Intent on winning, he constantly reminded the tutfo of the race but the bird would never listen to him.

True to its nature, the snake darted straight as an arrow down to the plains without looking left or right, intent on reaching the destination. Following the snake, Rongnyu was soon in sight of

> the plains. She knew she had won the race, but her happiness gave way to concern as she waited and waited for her lover.
>
> When Rangeet eventually rolled out from a steep mountain crag, he sighted Rongnyu far below him. He raged swiftly, pulling huge chunks of mud to reach the destination ahead of his lover. But Rangeet was already there. His first words on seeing her were, "*Thi-see-tha* (When did you arrive)?" When he realized he had come in second, his pride was hurt. It was intolerable! A trick of fate! Enraged because he had lost the race to a female, Rangeet decided to *flow back to the Himalayas.* He cried and groaned, threw himself on the ground and struck himself with such force that *he began to flow back* to the Himalayas causing destruction everywhere.......

See the continuations of this "love-story."

A slight different variation of this myth is to be found in J. R. Subba, *Mythology of the Peoples of Sikkim*, New Delhi, 2009, pp. 391–393. And a very similar folktale is found in Nepal. See Kesar Lall, *Gods and Mountains: The Folk Culture of a Himalayan Kingdom*, Nepal, Jaipur, New Delhi, 1991, p. 83.

Here we may add William Crooke's very pertinent comment in his *Religion and Folklore of Northern India,* New Delhi, 1925, p. 63:

> Many saints or holy men are supposed to possess the power of changing the courses of rivers. A Rishi changed the course of the Sarju; Bhrigu, the sage, gave to one of his disciples the power to drag the Narbada after him by trailing his clothes behind his back, on condition that he did not move as far as he wished; a Khasi tale tells how two goddesses changed the courses of two rivers. Anyone who has seen the remarkable changes in the courses of Indian rivers will understand the origin of stories such as these.

55. Dog-Faced People

In *B. Sanhedrin* 96a, referring to *Isaiah* 39:1 (= 2 *Kings* 20:12) where we read of Merodach-Baladan the son of Baladan, king of Babylon, that "Baladan the King had his face changed so that it looked like that of a dog." Or in other words, he became dog-headed. L. Ginzberg, in his *The Legends of the Jews*, vol. 6, Philadelphia, 1928, p. 368, note 82, writes:

> Baladan's dog-face is very likely a Jewish "explanation" of the dogs seen on Assyrian-Babylonian monuments in the company of Merodach. Comp. Roscher's *Lexicon der Mythologie* vol. 2, 2371.

Whether or not Ginzberg's explanation is correct, the meaning of the Talmudic statement is clearly meant to indicate that he was punished to look like some primitive creature. Certainly "dog-headedness" was a negative attribute like depravity among Talmudic sages, as in *B. Sanhedrin* 97a.

Rudolf Wittkower, in his *Allegory and the Migration of Symbols*, New York, 1977, in a wonderful chapter/essay, entitled "Marvels of the East: A Study in the History of Monsters" (first published in the *Journal of the Warburg and Courtauld Institute*, vol. 5, 1942), pp. 54–55, in discussing medieval maps which included pictures of fabulous animals distributed over the globe, gives the following example:

In the Hereford map (13 cent.)[46] there appear under the inscription 'Gigantes' two dog-headed men facing each other in a symmetrical group;[47] it is clear that instead of talking they are barking at each other. Now the fabulous races form part of Arabic illuminated manuscripts also. Manuscripts of Kazwini's in Munich.[48] According to the sources the cynocephali have no articulate speech and express themselves by barking. The grouping together of two of them is a typical pictorial creation to bear out this idea, and it cannot be doubted that the same prototype lies behind the Kazwini and the Hereford pictures. This prototype must ultimately have been Greek;[49] it spread on the one hand through Byzantium to the East, and possibly

46. [His note 97, on p. 200]: Cf. Konrad Miller, *Mappae Mundi. IV. Die Herefordkarte*, Stuttgart, 1896. W. L. Bevan and H. W. Phillott, *Mediaeval Geography. An Essay in Illustration of the Hereford Mappa Mundi*, London, 1873, is still very useful.

47. [His note 103, ibid.]: There was a tradition which identified the cynocephali with the giants. Cf. Klinger, p. 119 ff. Cristophorus, the giant, was said to be a cynocephalus, "Sanctus de Cynocephalorum oriundus genere" (*Acta Sanctorum*, July 25, p. 139), cf. also Ratramnus' *Epistola de Cynocephalis* (*P. L.* CXXI, c. 1155); P. Saintyves, "Saint Christophe successeur d'Anubis, d'Hermès et d'Héraclès," *Revue anthrop.* XLV, 1935, mainly p. 319 ff. In Isidore (XI, 3, 13–15) the description of the cynocephali follows immediately after giants. The cynocephali proper appear on the Hereford map in the north of Europe (cf. Miller, p. 18), also as a barking group but sitting. The northern tradition goes back to Aethicus c. 28, p. 15. Cf. the material collected by Wuttke, *Aethicos, op. cit.*, p. XIX ff.

See also the remarks in *The Travels of Marco Polo: The Complete Yule-Cordier ed.*, New York-Cordier 1893, vol. 2, p. 309, on the cynocephali of the Andaman Islands, and pp. 311–312, that the story originated … "in the disgust with which the 'allophylian' types of countenance are regarded, kindred to the feelings which makes Hindu and other Eastern nations represent the aborigines whom they superseded as demons." And cf. ibid., p. 228, note 3, on the "Dog-Headed Barbarians" or "Hill People…", by F. Ohlinger, in *Chinese Recorder*, July 1886, pp. 265–268. See also Cordier's note on pp. 109–110 (to chapter XIII, p. 311), with additional material.

48. [His note 104]: Cod. Arab. 464, f. 211v. This is the earliest Kazwini MS known to us, written in 1280; cf. Buchtal-Kurz-Ettinghausen in *Ars Islamica* VII, 1940, p. 162.

49. [His note 106]: The group may have a still older pedigree, being perhaps derived from a Babylonian "antithetical" model. Saxl in *Islam* III, 1912, p. 151 ff. could

> through illustrations on Roman maps to the West.[50] A very similar cynocephali group is to be found again in the tympanum at Vézelay. The monsters are here arranged with less rigid symmetry, but they still reveal the same source of inspiration as the Hereford and Kazwini groups.

Already earlier on in this essay he had noted the classical source for this motif. So he writes (p. 46) as follows in the section entitled "The sources of Indian monsters":

> It was the Greeks who were responsible for the western conception of India. The earliest surviving report of India is by Herodotus.[51] But his knowledge of that country was scanty and vague. About fifty years later, at the beginning of the 4th century BC, a special treatise on India was published by Ktesias from Knidos who had resided as royal physician at the court of Artaxerxes

---

retrace the representations of planets in Kazwini's cosmography to Babylonian sources.

50. [His note 107, p. 201]: It is, of course, not impossible that the type reached the West through Byzantine MSS, but none of the western MSS show the cynocephali as a group. Cf. Tikkanen, *Die Psalterilluster, im Mittelalter*, p. 56; Strzygowski, *Der Bilderkreis des griech. Physiologus*, p. 85; Dalton, *Byzant. Art and Archeology*, 1911, p. 161.

51. [His note 2, on p. 196]: Bk. IV, 44. Herodotus' other remarks about India are condensed in Bk. III, 97-106. Herodotus wrote his *History* towards the end of the fifth century BC. His account on India was probably based on that of Hekataios of Miletus (written about 500 BC) who in his turn drew on Skylax's report of a journey made c. 515 BC.

    The classical sources about India have been collected, translated, and commented upon in different works published by J. W. McCrindle. His sections dealing with Herodotus are in *Ancient India as described in Classical Literature*, Westminster, 1901, p. 1 ff. Cf. also the article Herodotus in *Paulys Real-Encyclopädie*, Suppl. II, 1913, c. 430. On the earliest Greek sources about India cf. Wilhelm Reese, *Die griechischen Nachrichten über Indien*, Leipzig 1914. Christian Lassen, *Ind. Alterthumskunde*, Bonn, 1849, II, p. 621 ff. "Geschichte des griech. Wissens von Indien" is still very useful. For the first part of this article cf. also H. G. Rawlinson, *Intercourse between India and the Western World. From the earliest Times to the Fall of Rome*, Cambridge, 1926.

> Mnemon of Persia.[52] Apart from numerous fragments transmitted by later authors his work has unfortunately only survived in an abridged version of the 9th century AD by Photios, the patriarch of Constantinople, who had probably a still stronger predilection for marvels than Ktesias himself.
>
> In any case, it is certain, owing to Ktesias' book, India became stamped as the land of marvels. He repeated all the fabulous stories about the East which had been current from Homer's time onwards and added many new ones, including tales of the weather, of miraculous mountains, diamonds, gold, etc. He populated India with the pygmies, who fight with the cranes;[53] with the sciapodes, a people with a single large foot on which they move with great speed and which they also use as a sort of umbrella against the burning sun;[54] and with the cynocephali, the men with dogs' heads "who do not use articulate speech but bark like dogs"[55]....

See also ibid., pp. 73–83, that Fra Oderic knew of dog-faced people living on an island near India, and such are illustrated in the German edition of Mandeville's Travels, Augsberg, 1492.

But there were not only dog-eared people, but also those whose

---

52. [His note 3, ibid]: Cf. J. W. McCrindle, *Ancient India as described by Ktesias the Knidian*, 1882; Reese, *op. cit.*, p. 7 ff. Ktesias returned to Greece in 398/397 BC where he wrote his *'Ινδιχά*. Cf. article Ktesias in *Paulys Ral-Encycl.* XXII, 1922, mainly c. 2037f.

53. [His note 4]: This famous story appeared first in the *Iliad* III, 6. Herodotus III, 116, IV, 13, although himself incredulous reported on the authority of Aristeas' *'Αρμάσπεια* that the one-eyed Arimaspi, inhabitants of the North, were the enemies of the griffins, and said that the Scythian word Arimaspi means "people with one eye" (IV, 27). Both traditions remained alive and reached the Middle Ages which represented either a dwarf-like race or cyclopes as fighting the birds.

54. [His note 5]: For earlier references to the sciapodes by Skylax, Hekataios and Herodotus cf. Reese, *op. cit.*, p. 49. Pliny VII, ii, 23 calls this race also Monocoli and this name remained the alternative for Sciapodes.

55. [His note 6]: Ktesias gave the first elaborate account of this people.

feet turned backwards.[56] Also headless people, who had faces in their chests are also cited in Wittkower, pp. 67, 69, 85. We are reminded of the Bhāts of India, the most dangerous of which is the Barham, or Brahma Rākshasa, a ghost of a Brahman who died a violent death. For "such spirits .... Are especially powerful and malicious. Sometimes they are represented as a headless trunk, with the eyes looking from the breast."[57] Additionally, "some like the Chures... have their feet turned backwards."[58]

Thus many of the monstrous marvels of the East noted by Wittkower in that essay, and the following one (ibid., pp. 76–92) entitled "Marco Polo and the Pictorial Tradition of the Marvels of the East" (first published in *Oriente Poliano*, Rome, 1957), appear to have their sources in the folkloristic beliefs of India, many of which persisted and survived until modern times. And I would suggest that the dog-headed motif evolved out of tales of primitive Indian jungle-tribesman who had, to the Westerner, strange facial characteristics. Since we know of connections between India and the Jewish centers of the Middle East, it may well be that King Baladan's dog-face myth-legend was influenced by the Indian dog-faced-person theme.

---

56. Wittkower, ibid., pp. 60–61, notes 143–144 on p. 202, referring to Isid. Etym. 9:2, etc.

57. See W. Crooke, *The Native Races of the Northern India*, London, 1906, p. 24, citing E. A. Gait, *Report on the Census of Bengal* 1902. Such needless people also appears in the Alexander romances, e.g., *A Hebrew Alexander Romance according to Ms Heb – 671.5, Paris Biblioteque National*, ed. W. Jac. Van Bekkum, Groningen 1994, p. 145, alt. And see *Seder haDorot* by Yehiel Heilprin, vol. 1, Warsaw, 1876, p. 30, on Jewish traditions of such strange creatures.

58. W. Crooke, *The Popular Religion and Folklore of Northern India*, vol. 1, London, 1896, p. 238. And cf. p. 270 on the Churel, that sometimes she is fair in front and black behind, but she invariably has her feet turned round, heels in front and toes behind.... The Gira, a water-spirit of the Konkan, has his feet turned inwards (J. S. Campbell, *Notes on the Spirit Basis of Belief and Customs*, Bombay, 1885, p. 156), etc.

Dog-headed men from Kazwini's cosmography, 1280 (Munich, cod. arab. 464, f. 211v)

Dog-headed men from the Hereford Map, 13th century (Hereford Cathedral)

Dog-headed men from the tympanum of Vézelay, 12th century

Illustrations nos. 75–77 from Wittkower, ibid., pp. 54–55

Ardhanārīshvara
Gurjara-Pratihārā period, *c.* 7th century
From Rajasthan
Sandstone
Jhalawar, Archaeological Museum

In the Image of Man: India's perception of the universe through 2000 years of painting and sculpture, London, 1982, p. 216

56. The Swallowed Shroud

In *Sefer Hasidim*, sect. 451, ed. M. Margaliot, Jerusalem 1957, p. 310, ed. Gutmann (Elad, 2010?), p. 410 and note 2, we read that:

> When there is a plague in a city, those corpses are searched, for perhaps in some instances the corpse swallowed the shroud, which is dangerous....

(See my *JLC*, vol. 1, pp. 473, note 22, 508–509.)

This explains what D. S. Sasoon wrote in his *Masa Bavel*, Jerusalem, 1955, p. 241, in the name of R. Abdalla Somech, in his *Zivhei Tzedek*, Baghdad, 1904, vol. 2, p. 183, sect. 115[x], that in Baghdad in 1773, when they went to bury a certain woman, they found she had the shroud in her mouth. They came and told R. Tzalah Matzliah, who, at that time, was the head of the rabbinic court, and he told them that there was an early tradition that this would indicate that a plague would beset them for an extended period, and one had to slaughter the woman. At that time a brave individual turned up and said that if they paid him much money, he would slaughter the woman. He took a sharp knife, slaughtered the woman, and pulled the shroud out of her mouth. Clearly this tradition is based on the passage in *Sefer Hasidim*, but it is not clear why he had to slaughter the dead woman.

See further Moshe Shohat in *Hitzei Gibborim* 8, 2015, pp. 826–827.

It is most interesting to find the following in A. M. T. Jackson and R. E. Enthoven's *Folk Lore Notes I: Gujarat*, Bombay, 1914, pp. 220–221:

> The following tale related an occurrence said to have taken place not long ago in the village of Verad. The headman of the village who was a Rajput by birth but who had lost his caste owing to irregular conduct with a woman, died of fever, and as he was an outcaste his body was buried instead of being cremated. Soon after, a number of persons in the same village happened to die of the same fever and the people conjectured that the late patel's corpse must be lying in its grave with its face downwards *chewing the khahan* (*perhaps kaphan, i.e., the cloth in which a corpse is wrapped*). Many thought that the health of the village would not be restored until the corpse was replaced in the correct position with its face upwards and *unless the kaphan was taken out of its mouth*. But none ventured to do so, being dissuaded by the fear of meeting with a worse fate. But although they did not open the grave yet they arranged for certain vows to be taken in honour of the dead man, and that put a stop to the disease.

Cf. ibid., p. 181, note 816, for the source.

Furthermore, William Crooke, in his *Religion and Folklore of Northern India*, ed. R. E. Enthoven, New Delhi, 1925, p. 130, writes:

> Recently in the Deva Ismaïl District of the Panjab sickness was said to be due to the fact that a woman who had died some months before was chewing her shroud. It was determined to disinter the corpse, to place a copper coin in the mouth of the corpse, and a cock was killed and laid on her body…

We recognize the various motifs – elements, the swallowing of the shroud, the placing of a coin in the mouth (see my discussion in *JLC*, vol. 2, chapter 37) and the sacrifice of a cock, all of which have been combined.

I might have added (that which I noted in my *Addenda et Corrigenda* to *JLC*, vol. 1, pp. 752–753), that in Teutonic mythology, Persian customs, and even in the *Folk-Lore from Adams County, Illinois*, ed. Harry Middleton Hyatt, New York, 1935, p. 206, no. 4304, who claims this belief is "Jewish," I have found such references, and also among the Mandaeans. See E. S. Drower, *The Mandaeans of Iraq and Iran: Their Cults, Customs, Magic, Legends and Folklore*, 2nd ed., Leiden, 1962, pp. 185–186:

> Meanwhile, the digging of the grave is in process. The depth is not prescribed, but there must be a hollowed-out space behind the head, left unfilled with earth and called the *lahad* [Arabic "niche or cavity in a tomb"]. The corpse is then laid in the tomb, always facing the north, and a few stones are placed on the *rasta* of the dead man, and one on his mouth. The legend told to explain this is that once, after a man had died, his family began to die, too, one after the other. They went to the *ganzibra*, who counseled that they should dig up the man who had first died and examine the corpse. They did so, and found that the *kinzala* (stole) had been stuffed into the mouth of the corpse.

So apparently this is a widespread superstition found in a number of different cultural venues.

Conclusion

It is obvious we have not done more than scrape the surface of this area of research. Many tantalizing similarities may be found. Thus the Goddess Kali has a long tongue as a sort of punishment for her behavior towards her consort. And in *B. Sotah* 35a, R. Haninah bar Papa cites Rav Shelah of Kfar Tamra as saying that the spies that Moses sent to spy out the Land of Israel, and came back with bad reports (*Numbers* chapters 13–14), were punished in such a way "that their tongues were so lengthened that they reached unto their navels, and worms would come out of their tongues and enter through their navels [back] to their tongues..."

So too B. Heller in *REJ* 49, p. 190, suggested the legend of Palti in *B. Sanhedrin* 19b, according to which, he, Michal's second husband is highly praised for his control over his passion. For obeying King Saul's command he went through the ceremony of marriage with Michal, and as far as the outside world was concerned they lived as a married couple. But he never came near her, knowing that she was King David's lawful wife. And, as R. Yohanah states, he was called *Paltiel,* because he escaped (*palto*) from sin. "What did he do? He placed a sword between himself and herself, and said, Anyone [meaning himself] who has sexual relations with her will be slain with the sword." See L. Ginzberg, *The Legends of the Jews*, vol. 6, Philadelphia, 1928, pp. 273–274, note 133. However, Ginzberg rejects Heller's suggestion, comparing the phrase "he placed a sword ... will be slain with this sword" with a similar such phrase in *B. Shabbat* 17a and *B. Yevamot* 77a.

Furthermore, examples of such "similarities" may be found between Jewish and European legends such as the werewolf motif. For biblical Benjamin, on the basis of *Genesis* 49:27, is described as a werewolf changing from human to wolf by day and night.[59]

So folklore, and especially comparative folklore, is a labyrinth in which one can get hopelessly lost, but very pleasurably so.

---

59. So wrote Rabbenu Efraim, Jerusalem, 1992, to *Genesis*, ibid., verse 27 (p. 167) that:

> "Benjamin shall rave as a wolf" is not just a sort of simile, but that at times he would turn into a wolf and ravage people, and only when he was in the presence of his father Jacob, who had there a doctor, would he not turn into a wolf.

He goes on to explain (ibid.) that he was a person who turns into a wolf:

> And when he changed into a wolf, called *luf [lupo] garo*, his legs came out of his shoulders, as it is written and he [Benjamin] shall dwell between his shoulders" (*Deuteronomy* 33:12). And this is how he was cured of being a wolf: when he entered a house and a person was afraid of him, he would gather up the ashes left in the fireplace and throw them here and there, and the person would not be harmed. And this is what was done daily in the Temple, that the ashes next to the altar were thrown about, as it is stated, "[And the priest shall … take up the ashes …] and put them beside the altar" (*Leviticus* 6:3). And this was the way of a person who changed into a wolf. For a wolf was born with fangs, that is to say to devour the world …, and even when he changes into a man, [nonetheless] he always has a tail. So too, a strip went out of the portion of Benjamin [in the Land of Israel], and it entered into the portion of Judah, and on it was the Temple.

(Cf. *B. Megillah* 26a.) See also Wolf Zichermann, *Otzar Plaot ha-Torah, Genesis*, Brooklyn, 2013, pp. 544, note 3, pp. 609–610, note 124.

On the werewolf motif, see, e.g., Claude Lecouteaux, *Witches, Werewolves and Fairies*, transl. Clare Frock, Rochester, VT, 1992; Frank Hamel, *Werewolves, Bird-Women, Tiger-Men and Other Human Animals*, Mineda, NY 1917; Sabine Baring-Gold, *The Book of Werewolves*, London, 1865; Robert Eisler, *Man into Wolf: An Anthropological Interpretation of Sadism, Masochism, and Lycanthropy*, London (n.d. but circa 1949), etc.

Afterword

Since the late '50s and early '60s, when I visited and even lived for a while in India, I have been enthralled, perhaps even bewitched, by that fascinating country/sub-continent, with its history, religions, mythologies, and great variety of manners, beliefs, and superstitions; or, in other words, by its ideologies, sociology, and anthropology. Since those early days I have lived, as it were, with one foot firmly rooted in my authentic Jewish heritage, and the other tentatively dipping into those captivating magical waters of India. And, at times, peering into those rippled waters I see images which remind me if not of myself, then something mysteriously similar. These undulating ripples with their tantalizing almost-reflections somehow gave rise to this little book, a book of fleeting double images, as though from a slightly unfocused camera lens. These almost-parallels serve as a sort of mental itch, raising questions as yet unanswered but which are not for me to resolve.

Appendix

Some Comments on Indo-Judaic Etymology

By Daniel Sperber

Many years ago, I met with Prof. Chaim Rabin in London,[60] and asked him whether there were early contacts with India and Israel, and I meant contacts with Jews in general. "Well," he replied, "already the Hebrew Bible contains certain Sanskrit and Tamil words, such as, for example, cinnamon, emerald, sapphire and topaz, suggesting trade contacts already in Solomon's time. And the word tuki (peacock) in 1 Kings 10:22 (= 2 Chronicles 9:21) is actually a Dravidian 'loanword.'" That triggered off for me a great interest in that subject, some of the results of which I should like to present here.

In modern Hebrew *tuki* is a parrot. But the biblical *tuki* is a peacock. Cf. Malabar: *tōgai, tōghai* – peacock, Gesenius – Robinson, BOB, Oxford 1906, p. 1067a s.v. תוכיים. However, see A. A. Macdonell and A. Berriedale Keith, *Vedic Index of Names and Subjects*, London, 1958, pp. 432, especially note 14, who are doubtful of this etymology though they do seem to equate Sanskrit *kapi* with Hebrew *kof* – monkey. *Kapi* as a monkey appears in *RV* 10:86.5, see ibid., vol. 1, p. 136, s.v. I *kapi*, with bibliography.

60. Many years later, after his disease, his wife Batya (Betty), whom I knew from London, gave me some of his books with his annotations, such as the two volumes of Johannes Friedrich's *Hethitisches Wörterbuch*, Heidelberg, 1952 and 1957; Pokorny's *Indogermanisches Etymologisches Wörterbuch*, Bern and Munich, 1959, 1969; Horn's *Grundriss der Neupersischen Etymologie*, Strassburg, 1893, etc.

Alexis Soyer, in his *The Pantophaean, or A History of Food and its Preparation in Ancient Times*, London, 1853, p. 166, writes:

> The peacock comes originally from India: it was there that Alexander the Great saw it for the first time. He was so struck with its magnificent plumage that he forbade all persons, under penalty of death, to kill any (Nornias 2:24, early 1 cent. C.E.).

(His other reference on p. 425 n. 115 is to Aldrovandi 13:1; I presume he is referring to the 16 cent. Scientist Ulysses Aldrovandi, in one of his many works. But I have not succeeded in identifying it.)

Soyer continues (ibid.):

> These birds were … known over various parts of the world. Samos, which seems to have provided one of the first, ornamented its money with their image (Varro *R. R.* 3:6; *Athenaeus* 14:9.25). Their reputation spread far and wide, and Athenian speculators sent to that island for peacocks, which were shown to the curious once a month (*Aelian* 6:21).[61]

See also *The Travels of Sir John Mandeville*, Dover ed., New York, 1964, pp. 142, 348; Edward H. Schafer, *The Golden Peaches of Samarkand: A Study of T'ang Exotics*, Berkeley, Los Angeles, London, 1963, index, p. 393, s.v. Peacock; but especially p. 96, that "before the Man dynasty, the only pea fowl know to the Chinese was the Indian peacock" (*T'ang sha* 37, 37 21a).

Prof. Rabin also gave me his article published in *Proceedings of the Second International Seminar on Tamil Studies*, Madras, 1971, pp. 432–440, entitled "Loanword Evidence in Biblical Hebrew for Trade between Tamiland and Palestine in the First Millennium B.C."; and later I came upon his "Lexical Borrowings from Indian Languages

---

61. See J. W. McCrindle, *The Invasion of India by Alexander the Great...*, Westminster, 1903, pp. 362–363, note Aa, that the peacock (*mayûra*) abounds in India, especially in the forests at the foot of the Himalaya. See also, idem. *Ancient India as Described in Classical Literature*, Westminster, 1901, p. 139, citing *Aelian* ibid.

as Carriers of Ideas and Technical Concepts," *Between Judaism and Banares; Comparative Studies in Judaism and Hinduism*, ed. Hananya Goodman, New York, 2012, etc. See also his *Hikrei Lashon: Asufat Maamarim bi-Leshon ha-Ivrit u-be-Ahioteha*, ed. M. Bar Asher and Barak Dan, Jerusalem, 1999, pp. 304–305: *tokai* in Tamil. There he also shows that the rabbinic *tavas*, peacock, is related to Tamil *tabos*, Greek *taōs*, etc., while in ibid., p. 175, he also lists the following Hebrew words with Indian origin, such as *anach*, plumb-line (Jastrow, *Dictionary*, vol. 1, 85b) – nāga, Armenian *oneg*, lead; *bedil – paṭira*, lead; *bareket – marahata*, jewel, morning star (Jastrow, *Dictionary*, vol. 1, 197ab); *kinnor* (biblical Hebrew) – *kimnara* (loanword from Telugu); *karkom – kurkuma*, cf. Persian *kurkum*; *karpas* (form of cloth, biblical) – *karpasa*, cotton; *nadan* (biblical Hebrew) – *nidhana*, sheath; *sapir - šanipriya*, though it would appear that the Sanskrit is a modern term; see E. Masson, *Recherches sur les plus anciens emprunts sémitiques en grec*, Paris, 1967, p. 66, note 2; *pitda – pîta*, topaz (see E. H. Warmington, *The Commerce between the Roman Empire and India*, London 1928, pp. 242, 247–249, 259–260, 353, 383 n. 80, on topaz and sapphire).

Each of these entries require much further examination and careful dating. As to *karkom* see also Laufer, *Sino-Iranica*, Chicago, 1910, p. 321; *barefeet*; idem, ibid., pp. 518–519, that Sanskrit *marakato* is actually of Semitic origin, *barrakatee* appearing in a Babylonian text of the 4 cent. B.C.E. (C. Fossey, "Etudes assyriennes," *Journal Asiatique* 1, 1917, p. 473). And as to the peacock, see Edward H. Schafer, ibid., London, 1963, pp. 96–99, 303–304, notes 43–71. The "gold peach" (Chinese *hwan t'ao*) was introduced into China from ancient Sogdiana – the capital of which is now Samarkand – in the seventh century C.E. The yellow peach, the size of a goose egg, was golden in color; hence its name, see B. Laufer, *Sino-Iranica*, Chicago, 1910, p. 379; Schafer, ibid., pp. 1, 279, notes 1, 117, 121.

And, of course, later on I became acquainted with S. D. Goitein and Mordechai A. Friedman's seminal Genizah studies on the "India Book," entitled *India Traders in the Middle Ages: Documents from the Cairo Geniza: "India Book,"* Leiden, Boston, 2008, and also

Louis Isaac Rabinowitz's *Jewish Merchant Adventures: A Study of the Radanites*, London, 1948.

However, further study has shown that there are, in fact, very few direct linguistic connections between Hebrew and Sanskrit. There are, however, Hebrew words which have some sort of connection with Sanskrit, but usually through the medium of Old Persian. Thus, the "Hebrew" *nērd* (*Canticles* 4:14), Greek *nardos* (Theophrastus, *Hist. Plant.* 9:7:2), Persian *nard* and *nārd*, are all derived from Sanskrit *nalada* (Prakrit: *nidhana*, Rabin, *Asufat*, pp. 175, 280), which already appears in the *Atharvaveda* (Macdonell and Keith, *Vedic Index* 2, p. 437), but probably came through the Persian. This was also noted by M. Casevitz, in his article "'Mots Voyageurs' From India to Greece," apud *Athens, Aden, Arikamedu: Essays on the interrelations between India, Arabia and the Eastern Mediterranean*, eds. Marie-Françoise Boussac and Jean-François Salles, New Delhi, 1995, p. 25 (and one may wonder whether *rewo*, meaning lion, can be related to Hebrew *ari – arie*, lion, see Casevitz, ibid., pp. 24–25). See Laufer, ibid., pp. 428, 455, and Warmington, ibid., index, s.v. nard, spikenard p. 409. Similarly, Hebrew *egoz* (*Canticles* 6:11) is related to Sanskrit *ākhōta*, which, however, appears to be an early Iranian loanword which penetrated into Sanskrit. Laufer (ibid., p. 248) notes that in the Hindu-Kush language Yidgha, the form *ogūzo* is to be found, and he compares it with New Persian *koz* and *goz*. (Cf. ibid., pp. 254, 256, note 1: Arabic *joz*, Kurd. *gwiz*, Pūštu *ughz*, *waghz*.) It is interesting to note that both the words we have mentioned come from *Canticles*, which according to Jewish tradition was written by King Solomon, who according to much later Aggadic sources had some connections with India. See, e.g., Louis Ginzberg, *The Legends of the Jews*, vol. 4, Philadelphia, 1954, p. 149, vol. 6, Philadelphia, 1946, p. 291, note 49. See further ibid., vol. 5, Philadelphia, 1955, p. 60, note 190, on the Indian origin of a Rabbinic tale.

Furthermore, Hebrew *kitan, kutna*, cotton, from Arabic *quṭn* or *quṭun*, may also have an Indian origin (cf. Lokosch, *Etym*, *Wörterbuch*, no. 1272), but this is by no means certain. See, in detail, Paul

Pelliot, *Notes on Marco Polo*, vol. 1, Paris, 1959, pp. 426–427, and Warmington, ibid., pp. 210–211, and in the index, s.v. cotton, p. 401.

And so too the later Hebrew (Talmudic) *pilpel* – pepper, Greek *peperi*, Latin *piper*, is surely derived, perhaps indirectly, from the Indian *pippali*. See Christian Lassen (1800–1876), *Indische Atherthumskunde*, vol. 2, Bonn, 1849–1852, p. 278, and reject Jastrow's derivation (in his *Dictionary*, vol. 2, p. 1184b, s.v. 1010, Ben Yehuda, p. 4963, s.v., etc.). The interchange between R and L is common, e.g. *garin* – *galin* – seed in biblical Hebrew, and cf. S. Krauss' *Lehnwörter*, vol. 1, Berlin, 1896, p. 111, no. 197. See further Laufer, ibid., p. 375, who writes that the Sanskrit *pippali* is attributed to Sasanian Persian Chinese source (*Cou šu*, chapter 50, p. 6). To this he adds:

> This pepper must have been also imported into Iran from India, for it is a native of the hotter parts of India from Nepal eastward to Assam the Khasia hills and Bengal westward to Bombay, and southward to Travancore, Ceylon, and Malacca. It is therefore surprising to read in the *Pen ts'ao* of the T'ang that *pi-po* grows in the country Po-se: this cannot be Persia, but refers solely to the Malayan Po-se. For the rest, the Chinese were very well aware of the Indian origin of the plant, as particularly shown by the adoption of the Sanskrit name. It is first mentioned in the *Nan fań ts'ao mu čwań*, unless it be there one of the interpolations in which this work abounds, but it is mixed up with the betel pepper (*Chavica betel*).

See also George Watt (1851–1936), *The Commercial Products of India*, London, 1908, p. 91 (and cf. in his *The Dictionary of Economic Products of India*, vol. 6/1, 1892, s.v.); E. H. Warmington, ibid., p. 410b, index, s.v. pepper. Warmington's book is extremely important for an understanding of the relations between India and the West. See also Strabo 2:5.12, 17:1.13, Pliny, *Hist. Nat.*6:101; 4:104–106; *Periplus Maris Erythraei* 41:5; *P. Vinch G.* 40822 (apud Casson, *ZPE* 84, 1990, p. 195); M. P. Charlesworth, *Trade Routes and Commerce of* *the Roman Empire*, 1926, p. 291a, index, s.v. India; V. K. Jain, *Trade and Traders in Western India*, Delhi, 1990; H. P. Ray, "The Western Indian Ocean and early maritime links of the Indian Subcontinent," *The Indian Economic and Social History Review* 31, 1994; R. Thapar, "Black Gold: South Asia and Roman Maritime Trade," *South Asia* 15/2, 1992, pp. 1–27; H. P. Ray, "A Resurvey of 'Roman' Contacts with the East," *Athens, Aden, Arikamedu…*, pp. 97–184; J.-F. Salles, "The Periplus and The Gulf," ibid., pp. 135–146; A. Tchernia, "Rome and India – Archeology Alone," ibid., pp. 147–156, being a review of V. Begley and R. D. De Puma, eds., *Rome and India: The Ancient Sea Trade*, University of Wisconsin Press, 1991, etc.

We may further add that since much of the spice and incense trade come to Europe and the West from the East – India and China – it is hardly surprising to find in European renaissance art that the East is symbolized as a figure holding a thurible with aromatic fumes, or a censer of myrrh or other similar spices. See, e.g., Rodney Shirley, *Courtiers and Cannibals, Angels and Amazons: The Art of the Decorative Cartographic Titlepage*, The Netherlands 2009, pp. 46–47; no. 9, Ortelius I, *Theatrum Orbis Terrarum* 1570; ibid., pp. 90–91; no. 27, Gerard Mercator and Jodocus Hondius, *Atlas…* 1575, ibid., pp. 188–189; no. 72, Pierre Mortier, *Atlas Novum* 1695; pp. 200–201; no. 76, Henri Abraham and Zacharias Chatelain, *Atlas Geographicus* 1708, pp. 246–247; no. 97, Robert Montgomery Martin, *The British Colonies* 1849 (Asia, an oriental with a spring of balsam in his hand), etc. For a brief, but comprehensive summary on the Indian spice trade, see the article by Stuart Cary Welch, "Encounters with India: Land of Gold, Spices and Matters Spiritual," apud *Circa 1492*: *Art in the Age of Exploration*, ed. J. A. Levenson, Yale University Press, New Haven and London, 1991, pp. 363–366. See also Ranabir Chakravarti, "Reaching Out to Distant Shores: Indo-Jewish Trade Contacts (up to C.E. 1300)," apud *Indo-Judaic Studies in the Twenty-First Century*, ed. N. Katz, New York, 2007, pp. 19–43, with rich bibliographic information.

On the Indian pepper (*piper*) tree, see also *The Etymologies of Isidore of Seville* (VI cent. C.E.), transl. S. S. Barney, W. J. Lewis, J. A. Beale, O. Berghot, Cambridge 2010, XVII, VIII, 8, p. 349.

We might add to the above the Hebrew word זוג – *zug*,- pair, couple, found in Mishnaic sources, e.g., *M. Eruvin* 9:10, etc. See *Ben Yehuda*, vol. 3, p. 1301, who in note 1, ibid., points out that this word appears in Arabic, and scholars have linked it to the word in Greek ζυγόν (*zugon*), yoke of a plow, etc., which links *two* oxen, etc. E. Neufeld, in his *The Hittite Laws*, London, 1951, p. 85, also pointed out this connection, but also to Hittite: yukam = yoke, Sanskrit *yugam*, Latin *iugum*, Greek ζυγος. In the *Etymological Dictionary of Greek* by Robert Beekes, Leiden, 2009, vol. 1, pp. 502–503, s.v. ζυγόν, we read:

> Old name of a device, retained in most Indo-European languages, e.g. Hittite *iugan*, Sanskrit *yugam*, Latin *ingum*....

He refers us to T. Pokorny, *Indogermanisches Etymologisches Wörterbuch*, vol. 1, Bern and Munich, 1959, pp. 509 et seq., etc. The connection between the Indo-European word and the Hebrew-Arabic *zug* is quite tantalizing.

Oddly enough, I did not find a discussion of the Hebrew *zug*, in Joseph Yehudah's *Hebrew is Greek*, Oxford, 1982, p. 471, or elsewhere in his book.

We may also call attention to the more complex problem of the Greek μεθυω. Robert Beekes, ibid., vol. 2, p. 919 s.v. μέθυ, who relates the etymology to Sanskrit *madhu*, honey, like the English "mead," which is retained in many Indo-European languages, e.g., Lithuanian *medus*, etc.; and see the discussion of Francesca Shiron, *From Alexandria to Babylon: Near Eastern Languages and Hellenistic Erudition in Oxyrhrynchus Glossary (P.Oxy. 1802+4812)*, Berlin, New York, 2009, p. 87, who writes:

> Can this be related to the Hebrew *matok*, Assyrian *matuq*, honey?

See *Ben Yehuda*, vol. 7, p. 3453b and ibid., note 5; *Von Soden*, vol. 2, p. 6336, s.v. *matuq*(*m*), etc. Note that Shironi wrote (ibid.) that "there is also (in the Ancient Letters) *md'k* wine, formed with the suffix *-*ka*."

I also found that *Darya*, Persian for sea or lake, Old Persian *draya*, *zraya* in Avestan, *drayā* or *zrēh* in Middle Persian – Pahlevi, has been tentatively connected with Judeo-Persian דריאה in *Isaiah* 8:23. See Paul Horn *Grundriss der Neupersischen Etymologie*, Strassburg, 1883, p. 125 no. 561 *deryā*. Hermann Möller, in his *Indoeuropaeisk-Semitisk Sammenlignende Glossarium*, Copenhagen, 1909, p. 23, s.v. dh-r, refers us to the Hebrew טרד (*tarad*) to drip, (Jastrow, *Dictionary*, p. 550a, s.v.), from Semitic **t-r-*, *+d-*, citing Arabic parallels. But this seems to me to be somewhat far-fetched.

We may further note that the biblical *Yavan*, Greece (*Genesis* 10:4; *Ezekiel* 27:13; *Zachariah* 9:13; etc.) is a "back-formation from the Prakit term *Yona* which is derived from the Old Persian from *Yauna* originally denoting the Ionian Greeks who were conquered by Darius in 545 B.C.E." See H. P. Ray, "The Yavanas in India," apud *Athens, Aden, Arikamedu…*, p. 76.

He further notes (ibid.) that:

> It first occurs in the Behistun inscription of Darius I dated to 519 B.C.E., (D. C. Sircar, *Select Inscriptions Bearing on Indian History and Civilization*, Calcutta, 1964, p. 3). As the Ionian Greeks were the first to have come into contact with India, the term initially stood for them. It was gradually extended to include not only the Greeks of West Asia but any group of people coming from either West Asia or the Eastern Mediterranean (R. Thapar, *Ancient Indian Social History*, Orient Longman, 1978, p. 164) …..

See the whole of his very interesting article, pp. 75–95. Ray seems, however, to be unaware of the biblical *Yavan*. However, see also Laufer, ibid., pp. 211–212, note 4, on Annamese *Yavana*.

And while we are discussing Indo-Persian-Hebrew linguistic connections, I should like to call attention to a short note by a distant, tragically short-lived, relative of mine, Dr. Albert Ehrman (1933–1981), which was first published in *Orientalia* 50/2, 1981, p. 197, and reprinted in *Current Issues in Linguistic Theory* 58, Amsterdam, Philadelphia, 1988, p. 525. There on the origin of the word "scarlet" he wrote as follows:

> According to modern lexicography, the English word "scarlet" derives from Old French *escarlate* which derives from Persian *saqirlat*, "a dress dyed red," (K. Lokotsch, *Etymologisches Wörterbuch der Europäischen Wörter orientalischen Ursprung*, Heidelberg, 1927, p. 142, no. 1794). Persian *saqirlat* itself is then traced through an earlier series of Arabic, Latin, and Greek derivations none of which has any connection with either the dyeing process or the color red. What has, apparently, been overlooked by the lexicographers is the well-documented phenomenon that in ancient and medieval times, the Jews were the recognized masters of the dyeing trade in both the Near East and Roman Europe (I. Abrahams, *Jewish Life in the Middle Ages*, New York, 1969, pp. 217–219). Moreover, "red" was the preeminent color of the dyer's trade (see, e.g., *Exodus* 25:5, *Nachum* 2:4, *T. Mikvaot* 3.6). Now the word employed by Jews to denote "red dye" or "red paint" is Jewish Aramaic *siqrā*. Dean Herbert Paper of Hebrew Union College informs me (private communication) that Persian *saqirlat* is *not* an Old Persian word but rather a loanword imported into Persian. The proposed Arabic, Latin, and Greek derivations, as noted above, are unrelated to red-dyeing. Nothing, on the other hand, would be more natural than for the Persians to have adopted Jewish Aramaic *siqrā* and add thereunto the common Persian suffix *lat*. We can thus trace the odyssey of Jewish Aramaic *siqra* into Persian *saqirlat*, [and] into Old French *escarlate* [and] into modern English "scarlet."

He further pursued this "sakar" approach in two more short studies in *JQR* 69, 1979, pp. 233–235, 522–525, on the connections with *mascara* and mosquerate, massacre, and in *JBL* 97, 1979, pp. 572–573 (pp. 526–527), on Judas Iscariot and the Talmudic Abba Siqara (*B. Gittin* 56a), head of the revolutionary *sicarii*.

It is, indeed, accepted that Persian *sakirlat* is the ancestor of Mediaeval Latin *scarlatum*, Old French *escalate*, English *scarlet*, although this too is by no means certain. See H. Yule and A. C. Burnell, *Hobson-Jobson: The Anglo-Indian Dictionary*, London, 1886, p. 861a, s.v. *Surlat,* that the form *sakirlah* must not be trusted to. It is a modern form, probably taken from the European word, according to Skeat (*The Concise Dictionary of English Etymology*, p. 417a, s.v. Scarlet), the Turkish *iskarlat* merely having been borrowed from the Italian *scarllato*. Skeat in his *An Etymological Dictionary of the English Language*, revised ed. Oxford 1909, p. 539, s.v., refers us to J. T. Zenker, *Dictionnaire Turc-Arabe-Persia*, Leipzig, 1886–1887, p. 49. However, *sakirlat* has nothing to do with Hebrew *sakar* ,(סקר) which, in turn, has no connection with biblical *sakar* (שקר), contra Jastrow, *Dictionary*, vol. 2, p. 1021a, s.v. סקר II. Likewise, the Persian word is unrelated to the Chinese *sa-ha-la*, as demonstrated by Laufer, *Sino-Iranica*, p. 497. So, regretfully, I must state that all Ehrman's etymological suggestions may be rejected. See further Leo Wiener, *Contributions Toward a History of Arabico-Gothic Culture*, vol. 1, New York, 1917, pp. 273–274, on *scarlatum*.

Having mentioned sakar, see further M. Sokoloff, *A Dictionary of Jewish Babylonian Aramaic of the Talmudic and Geonic Periods*, Ramat-Gan, Baltimore and London, 2002, p. 829a s.v. 2 סקר, סקרתא, and his *Syraic Lexicon*, Indiana, New Jersey, 2009, p. 1041a, s.v. 3 סקר. For the relationship to Arabic and Persian, see Kohut, *Aruch Completum* vol. 6, p. 121, s.v. 1 סקר. However, the origin of the word "massacre" remains to this day of unknown origin (see C. T. Onions, ibid., p. 560a s.v.).

We should also note that early connections between Palestine and India are not unlikely, as there is ample evidence of trade connections directly between India and Egypt, certainly during the Ptolemaic era (323–30 B.C.E.), and even diplomatic contacts from c. 240 B.C.E., and during part of that period Egypt controlled Syria-Palestine. See

India and Egypt: Influences and Interactions, ed. Saryu Doshi and Mostaia El Abhedi, Marg Publications, Bombay, 1993, and especially Lutli A. W. Yehya'a chapter on "Trade Relations," pp. 52–63, and that of M. C. Joshi, on "Transmission of Ideas and Imagery," pp. 64–83.

Indeed one of Philo's nephews, Marcus Julius Alexander, was a long-distance trader with possible business links to India. See Ranabir Chakravati, "Reaching out to Distant Shores: Indo-Judaic Trade Contracts (Up to C.E. 1300)," *Indo-Jewish Studies in the Twenty-First Century – A View from the Margin*, ed. Nathan Katz, New York, 2007, pp. 28 et seq.

So too Clearchus of Soli, c. 300 B.C.E. who quotes Megasthenes as follows:

> Megasthenes, the writer who was a contemporary of Seleucus Nicator, writes in the third book of his *Indica*: "All the options expressed by the ancients about nature are found also among philosophers outside Greece, some among the Indian Brahmans and others in Syria among those called Jews."

See Menachem Stern, *Greek and Latin Authors on Jews and Judaism*, vol. 1, Jerusalem 1976, p. 46. And idem, vol. 2, Jerusalem 1980, p. 659, where he quotes Claudian, c. 400 C.E., who talks of "all the vain imaginings of India depicted on Jewish curtains." See editor's note, ibid., for full references, especially p. 659, note to line 357:

> *Iudaicis quae pingitur India velis:* For a suggestion that curtain-painting was an occupation of Alexandrian Jews, see T. Birt, *Rhein. Museum,* XLV (1890), pp. 491 ff. See also Juster, [*Les Juifs dans L'Empire Romain*, 1984] vol. 2, p. 306, n. 8; *The Christian Topography of Cosmas Indicopleustes,* ed. E. O. Winstedt, Cambridge, 1909, p. 121 = III, 70, ed. W. Wolska-Conus, I, Paris 1968, p. 511. For possibility, on the other hand, that the tapestries are designated "Jewish" because their subject-matter derived from the Bible, and not because of their Jewish

workmanship, see C. Roth, *Journal of the Warburg and Courtauld Institutes,* XVI (1953), p. 34, n. 3.

Returning to Prof. Rabin, we note that he also sought to prove that King Solomon's "Song of Songs" had its roots in ancient South Indian Love poetry; (see *The Anchor Bible* vol. 7c, *Song of Songs*, transl. and ed. Marvin H. Pope, New Haven, London, 1977, pp. 27 et seq.), while Prof. David Flusser, tried to show that early Rabbinic legends describing Abraham's discovery of the one true God, were influenced by the *Upanishads* (from the 6th to the 2nd cent. B.C.E.); see his "Abraham and Upanishads," *Judaism and the Origins of Christianity*, Jerusalem, 1988, p. 649.

See further Richard G. Marks, "Hindus and Hinduism in Medieval Jewish Literature," *Indo-Judaic Studies*, ibid., p. 58; Brian Weinstein, "Traders and Ideas: Indians and Jews," ibid., p. 50; Abraham Melamed, "The Image of India in Medieval Jewish Culture: Between Adoration and Rejection," *Jewish History* 20/3–4, 2006, pp. 299–314; David Shulman, "Is there an Indian Connection in the Sefer Yetzirah?" *Aleph* 2, 2002, ed. Gad Friedenthal, where there is a discussion of whether Saadya Gaon's apparent belief that there is an Indian influence on *Sefer Yetzirah* is likely or not, etc.

Over the years I have found a number of additional examples of the philological phenomenon of the possible linguistic connection (of some words) between Hebrew and Sanskrit. However, the direction of transmission and the medium through which such transmission may have taken place is often unclear. Thus, for example, Hebrew *kadkod* (כדכד)in *Ezekiel* 27:16, and *Isaiah* 54:11, seems to be related to Sanskrit *karkoda* (*karkatika*), a kind of mineral. See Manfred Mayrhofer, *A Concise Etymological Sanskrit Dictionary*, vol. 1, Heidelberg 1956, pp. 171–172, s.v. *karkocia.* Similarly *karmil* in 2 *Chronicles* 2:6, 13:3, 14, crimson, may be related to Sanskrit *kṛmiḥ*, a type of worm (Mayrhofer, ibid., pp. 261–262 s.v.). See too *karpas* (*Esther* 1:6), to *karpāsah* (ibid., p. 174 s.v.), and perhaps *kinnor*, ibid., s.v. *kimnarā*; *kusbara*, ibid., p. 249, s.v., *kustumbari*; *letaah* from *latē*, ibid., vol. 3, Heidelberg, 1976, p. 88, s.v.; etc.

And on *karpāsa-karpas*, see also W. H. Schoff, *The Periplus of the Erythræan Sea*, New York... 1912, p. 71.

However, similarity does not necessarily mean derivation. Thus, for example, one scholar wrote:

> Only a linguistic lunatic would derive *water* from [Hittite] *water*; the correspondence merely illustrates that Hittite is in some way related to the Indo-European languages...

And by the way compare Latin *lux*, light, with Hittite *lukzi*, light up.

Similarly Greek *pneu-*, breathe, blow, obviously has no connection with the American-Indian Klanath of Oregon, which has the verb *pniw*, "to blow." See Calvert Watkins, *The American Heritage Dictionary of Indo-European Roots*, Boston, New York, 2000, p. VIII. Furthermore, needless to say, this has nothing to do with biblical Hebrew *penimah*, inwards facing, *penimi*, inner.

There are probably some additional examples to be examined; however, as the subject requires a more extensive study, let the above suffice at this stage.

About the Author

Rabbi Professor Daniel Sperber is a leading scholar of Jewish law, customs, and ethics. He taught in the Talmud Department of Bar-Ilan University, where he also served as dean of the Faculty of Jewish Studies and president of the Jesselson Institute for Advanced Torah Studies. In 1992, he was awarded the Israel Prize for Jewish Studies. For close to five decades, Rabbi Sperber served in Jerusalem as rabbi, first at Yad Tamar Synagogue in Katamon and then at Menachem Zion Synagogue in the Old City. He now lives in Ovnat, a small settlement on the banks of the Dead Sea.

The descendant of a line of distinguished Orthodox rabbis, Prof. Sperber was born in 1940 in a castle in Ruthin, Wales, and studied in the Yeshivot of Kol Torah and Hevron in Jerusalem. He earned a BA in art history at the Courtauld Institute of Art and received a PhD in classics, ancient history, and Hebrew studies from University College, London.

In the mid-1960s, Prof. Sperber served as a rabbi in Calcutta, and he has visited India for a variety of reasons more than twenty times in the last sixty years.

Prof. Sperber has published some forty books and more than four hundred articles on the subjects of Talmudic and Jewish socio-economic history, law and customs, classical philology, and Jewish art. Among his major works is a well-known, eight-volume series, *Minhagei Yisrael*, on the history of Jewish customs. More recently, he has written books on halachic methodology and rabbinic decision-making in confrontation with modernity and has established an independent *beit din* dealing with *agunah* issues. He is the author of *On Changes in Jewish Liturgy: Options and Limitations*; *On the Relationship of Mitzvot Between Man and His Neighbor and Man and His Maker*; *The Importance of the Community Rabbi: Leading with Compassionate Halachah*; *Rabba, Maharat, Rabbanit, Rebbetzin: Women with Leadership Authority According to Halachah*; *Vegetarianism, Ecology, and Business Ethics: Three Essays of Judaic Insights into Contemporary Concerns*; and *History, Revolution, and Achievements of Nostra Aetate: The Second Vatican Council Declaration on the Relation of the Church with Non-Christian Religions*, all published by Urim Publications.